Badr al-Dīn Lu'lu'
Atabeg of Mosul, 1211-1259

Occasional Papers, Number 3

Middle East Center
Jackson School of International Studies
University of Washington

This book has been published with
the generous support of the
Farhat J. Ziadeh Fund for Arab and Islamic Studies
University of Washington

DOUGLAS PATTON

Badr al-Dīn Lu'lu'

Atabeg of Mosul, 1211-1259

Distributed by
University of Washington Press
Seattle and London

Printed in the United States of America

Cover design by Corinna Campbell

Library of Congress Cataloging-in-Publication Data

Patton, Douglas
Badr al-Dīn Lu'lu' : Atabeg of Mosul, 1211–1259 / Douglas Patton.
p. cm. -- (Occasional papers / Middle East Center of the Jackson School of International Studies, University of Washington ; no. 3)
Includes bibliographical references (p.) and index.
ISBN 0-295-97156-8
1. Mosul (Iraq)--History. 2. Lu'lu', Badr al-Dīn ibn ʿAbd Allāh, d. 1259. 3. Iraq--History--634-1534. 4. Islamic Empire--History--750-1258. I. Title. II. Series: Occasional papers (Henry M. Jackson School of International Studies. Middle East Center) ; no. 3.
DS79.9.M6P38 1991
956.7'4--dc20 91-27342
CIP

Distributed by
University of Washington Press
Seattle and London

For Amy

CONTENTS

ACKNOWLEDGMENTS

The following work has been my spare time labor for many years. I have been helped by many people—far too many to enumerate here in any meaningful way. I must, however, express my appreciation to the members of the University of Washington's Middle East Center for their support and encouragement. I am particularly grateful to Professors Jere Bacharach and Farhat Ziadeh for the enthusiasm they have shown for this project. I also want to thank my wife Amy for her support and editorial advice; wherever clarity has been achieved in the following pages it is entirely the result of her efforts. My son Tom, though too young to have made a direct contribution, inspired me with his energy and good humor.

Badr al-Dīn Lu'lu'
Atabeg of Mosul, 1211-1259

INTRODUCTION

At the time of his death in 657/1259, Badr al-Dīn Lu'lu' had ruled the city of Mosul for more than forty years.[1] During his remarkable career he rose from mamluk to sultan, usurping the throne of his master's descendants and establishing his rule in his own name. As an independent ruler, he exploited the growing weakness of the Ayyubid dynasty and expanded Mosul's dominion to an extent nearly as great as it had been a century before under the early Zangids. In his efforts to secure and expand his territory, he supported al-Ṣāliḥ Ayyūb, the Ayyubid ruler most dependent on mamluk power, and thereby indirectly fostered mamluk usurpation of Ayyubid rule in Egypt. He also cultivated the favor of the Mongols and willingly supported their invasion of Iraq, thus playing a role in the overthrow of the ʿAbbāsid Caliphate and the establishment of Mongol rule. Despite his important part in these dramatic transformations, Lu'lu' is today known almost exclusively as a patron of the arts and as Mosul's ruler during a period of great artistic brilliance.[2]

1. The principal secondary accounts of Lu'lu''s life are C. Cahen, "Lu'lu'"; Farès, 625–31; al-Jalabī; al-Ruwayshidī; Ṣā'igh, 199–200, 223–28; and Zettersté en.

2. His name is seldom omitted from studies of Islamic metalwork, manuscript illumination, epigraphy, and architecture. See the Bibliography under Farès, Rice (especially "The Brasses of Badr al-Din

The obscurity of Lu'lu''s political career does not arise from any lack of historical material. The medieval historians fully appreciated his importance, and repeatedly asserted that he was a handsome, youthful, energetic, and firm ruler, outstanding for his intelligence, shrewdness, and good administration (*siyāsa*). In the words of his contemporary Ibn Wāṣil, often repeated by later authors, "dirt did not touch him; the order of his realm was undisturbed."[3] His firmness was widely admired. Ibn al-Dawadārī reported that "no matter in his realm escaped him,"[4] and al-Dhahabī noted that "despite his tyranny and oppression, he was loved by his subjects because he treated them in a manner [which balanced] greed and fear."[5] Similarly, al-Yūnīnī (as cited by al-Dhahabī) said that he "could not be resisted by his amirs. He killed, hung, and cut unendingly until the land was deserted. Despite this, he was beloved by his subjects, who swore by his life, exaggerated his beard, and titled him Golden Wand (*qaḍīb al-dhahab*)."[6] Baybars al-Manṣūrī stated that "he was beloved by the people, approved by the elite; he promoted justice among his subjects."[7] Two centuries after his death, Ibn Taghribirdī gave him the ultimate tribute, saying: "may God

---

Lu'lu'"), Sarre, and van Berchem; also Étienne Combe, Jean Sauvaget and Gaston Wiet, eds., *Répertoire chronologique d'épigraphie arabe* (hereafter cited as *RCEA*).

3. Ibn Wāṣil, Bibl. Nat. MS 1702, f. 386b; Baybars al-Manṣūrī (Bodl.) f. 167a; Abu'l-Fidā, 6:104; al-Dhahabī, *Ta'rīkh al-Islām*, Bodl. MS Laud 305, f. 306a.

4. 8:45.

5. Al-Dhahabī, *Ta'rīkh al-Islām*, Bodl. MS Laud 305, f. 306a.

6. Ibid. This quotation is not found in the Hyderabad edition of al-Yūnīnī's *Dhayl mir'āt al-zamān*.

7. Br. Libr., f. 35b.

make such rulers plentiful. The people need a ruler like this to rule the entire world."[8]

While such fulsome praise is common in the royal biographies of the time, it is by no means showered on every ruler. Lu'lu' had qualities which distinguished him from the typical ruler of his time, and his conduct affected the policy of every court in the region. The present lack of appreciation for his political activity has many reasons, most notably the considerable historiographical difficulties encountered in the reconstruction and interpretation of the events of his reign. Ironically, these difficulties stem primarily from the success of one of Lu'lu''s most notable acts of patronage, for it is he who commissioned ʿIzz al-Dīn Ibn al-Athīr to write the *Kāmil fi'l-ta'rīkh*, which must be considered among the most influential world histories ever written.

Ibn al-Athīr's concern to justify his patron's legitimacy as ruler of Mosul and protector of the Zangids necessitated that he conceal an important aspect of the achievement: the usurpation of an established dynasty's authority by a mamluk slave. Ibn al-Athīr cannot be faulted for this approach. He wrote while the Zangids still retained nominal control of Mosul and his primary task was to assert his patron's worthiness to rule in their name. The historians of later eras understood more fully the significance of Lu'lu''s rise from mamluk to sultan, but their respect for the stature of Ibn al-Athīr and their reliance on his vivid narrative caused them to reinforce his glorious presentation of his patron. But for a few oblique references, the significance of Lu'lu''s accomplishment almost completely escapes their attention. This is particularly regrettable because of

8. 7:70.

the close parallel between the manner of Lu'lu''s rise to power and that of the mamluks of Egypt thirty years later.

While considerations of Ibn al-Athīr's stature and the context in which his history was written can offset the bias inherent in his account, the history of the latter half of Lu'lu''s reign has no such corrective. The fall of the Zangids certainly did not diminish Lu'lu''s importance as a ruler, but Ibn al-Athīr's death in 630/1233 left Mosul with no historian to chronicle and defend his actions. Estimations of Lu'lu''s stature must be based solely on the observations of historians working under other rulers in other cities. This severely limits our understanding of Lu'lu''s relations with the Mongols and the events leading to their occupation of Iraq. It is evident from all accounts that Lu'lu' enjoyed the trust of the Mongols and usually served them loyally, but the significance of his conduct may be seen only in terms of its immediate effect on the ruler or dynasty with whom each historian is primarily concerned. These historians are uninterested in his policy or motivation and record little about the evolution of the relationship, or why and how Lu'lu' came to be drawn into the Mongol orbit. Lu'lu''s actions, when mentioned at all, are usually described in simple and opportunistic terms appropriate to a subject of peripheral interest. Three distinct pictures emerge from the various accounts, depending on whether Lu'lu' is seen through the eyes of Ayyubid, Mamluk, or Mongol era historians.

Notwithstanding these limitations, it is clear that Lu'lu' was an important figure in the political history of his day, and that his influence was felt far beyond Mosul and long after his death. The exact nature of his significance is more clearly seen for the period of his rise to power, thanks to the perspective provided by Ibn al-Athīr. For the latter half of his career, the conjectures which are presented below are far less certain. Greater certainty will be achieved only as more work is done on the history and historiography of the period. It is hoped that the present research will contribute something to that end.

I

From Mamluk to Sultan

The Decline of Zangid Power

Badr al-Dīn Abu'l-Faḍā'il Lu'lu' b. 'Abd Allāh al-Nūrī al-Atābikī was the mamluk of Mosul's last independent Zangid ruler, the Atabeg Nūr al-Dīn Arslān Shāh (ruled 589–607/1193–1211).[1] Mosul's territory then extended only a score of miles beyond its wall, and was bordered by the small principalities of Irbil, Sinjār, and Jazīrat b. 'Umar. During the lifetime of the Ayyubid ruler Ṣalāḥ al-Dīn, the "eastern lands," as these principalities were known, came to be firmly subordinate to his authority. After his death in 589/1193, however, Ayyubid authority was weakened by the eruption of a bitter succession conflict, which was intensified by deep ethnic and regimental rivalries in the army.[2] Arslān Shāh was quick to capitalize on the Ayyubids' disunity and reassert Zangid independence. In the hope of winning Ayyubid recognition for his independence, he provided support to the Ayyubid ruler of Damascus, al-Afḍal, who was Ṣalāḥ al-Dīn's son

1. A different presentation of the material in this chapter is scheduled for publication in *Studia Islamica* under the title "Badr al-Dīn Lu'lu' and the Establishment of a Mamluk Government in Mosul."

2. 'Izz al-Dīn Ibn al-Athīr, *Al-Kāmil fi'l-ta'rīkh*, 12:341 (hereafter cited as *Kāmil*); Ibn al-Sā'ī, *Mu'allim*, f. 80b; Bar Hebraeus, 1:375; Ibn al-'Ibrī, 233; Ibn Wāṣil, 4:31.

and designated successor. Since al-Afḍal numbered among his supporters many who had been prominent in the government of the Zangid ruler of Syria, Nūr al-Dīn (ruled 541–69/1146–74), his cause was attractive to Arslān Shāh. Furthermore, certain influential families were represented by members in the courts of both rulers.[3] Because of al-Afḍal's reliance on such supporters, his victory could only have strengthened the newly regained independence of the Zangids.

The Ayyubid conflict was resolved by 598/1202, however, with the triumph of Ṣalāḥ al-Dīn's brother al-ʿĀdil, who conquered Egypt and Damascus and established his control over the army. By 606/1210 he had reimposed Ayyubid domination over the eastern lands, including the non-Zangid principalities of Mārdīn, Kharput, and Khilāṭ. Sinjār became the first Zangid city to acknowledge his supremacy in 600/1204.[4] Arslān Shāh at first resisted al-ʿĀdil's expansion; he invaded Sinjār when it submitted to al-Ādil, but was soon forced to abandon his efforts in the face of the overwhelming forces marshalled against him. Al-ʿĀdil's son al-Ashraf, in command of Ayyubid, Artuqid, and Irbili troops, easily drove Arslān Shāh from Sinjār. Arslān Shāh recognized the hopelessness of further opposition, and gave his sister Turkān Khātūn (d. 640) to al-Ashraf in marriage in 605/1208–9.[5] Thus all the eastern lands came to be subor-

3. Among them the al-Shahrazūrī family and the family of the historian Ibn al-Athīr. See Patton, "History of the Atabegs," 413–22, 431–33, 500–501.

4. Sinjār had dropped Ayyubid names from its coinage in 595 after the death of the Ayyubid ruler al-ʿAzīz ʿUthmān of Egypt. Al-ʿĀdil's name first appears with issues of the year 600. See Artuk, 421; Hennequin, 330–41; al-Ḥusaynī, 129–32; Lane-Poole, 3:224.

5. *Kāmil*, 12:284; Sibṭ, 337; Abū Shāma, 45–46; al-Birzālī, f. 418b; al-Dhahabī, *Taʾrīkh al-Islām*, Bodl. MS Laud 305, f. 149a; al-Ṣafadī,

dinate to al-ʿĀdil, who had unified the Ayyubid empire for the first time since the death of Ṣalāḥ al-Dīn.

Al-ʿĀdil now attempted what Ṣalāḥ al-Dīn had failed: the annexation of the Zangid states. He began with a surprise invasion of the Jazīra, laying siege to Sinjār in 606/1209.[6] The quarrelling rulers of the eastern states suddenly confronted the real possibility that al-ʿĀdil might annex their territories one by one. The threat forced Arslān Shāh and Muẓaffar al-Dīn Kūkburī, the ruler of Irbil, to put aside their differences and face the invasion together. To seal the alliance, the two sons of Arslān Shāh, Masʿūd and Zankī, married daughters of Kūkburī.[7] The alliance was further strengthened by the addition of the Rūm Saljuqs and the Ayyubid al-Ẓāhir Ghāzī of Aleppo, both of whom had sided against al-ʿĀdil during the recent civil war. The alliance prevented al-ʿĀdil from conquering the Jazīra, but the treaty of peace was on Ayyubid terms and required concessions from the Zangids. Sinjār had to cede the territory occupied by al-ʿĀdil, and Arslān Shāh was apparently required to proclaim Ayyubid supremacy on his coinage and in the

Al-Wāfī biʾl-wafayāt, vol. 10, ed. Ali Amara and Jacqueline Sublet, Bibliotheca Islamica, vol. 6j (Wiesbaden: Franz Steiner Verlag, 1400/1980), 380–81; Ibn Kathīr, 13:161–62.

6. The invasion of Sinjār: *Kāmil*, 12:284–87; Ibn Naẓīf, ff. 127b–29a (Doudou translation, 40–42); Sibṭ, 353; Ibn al-Sāʿī, *Muʿallim*, ff. 73a–b; Ibn Wāṣil, 3:190–95.

7. Kūkburī's wife and the mother of the brides was Rabīʿa Khātūn, a sister of al-ʿĀdil and Ṣalāḥ al-Dīn. See Ṭulaymāt, *Muẓaffar al-Dīn Kūkbūrī*, 63–65. On Rabīʿa Khātūn and the marriage see *Kāmil*, 12:287; Ibn al-Sāʿī, *Muʿallim*, f. 77b; Abū Shāma, 114; Ibn Khallikān, 4:121; 5:208; Ibn Wāṣil, 4:20, 114–15; 5:49–50; Ibn Kathīr, 13:136, 170–71.

khuṭba.[8] Arslān Shāh's efforts to negotiate a contract of marriage to a daughter of al-ʿĀdil may be seen as further evidence of his dependent status.[9]

It was at this time—when the Zangid revival had failed and Ayyubid authority was again recognized throughout the Jazīra—that Badr al-Dīn Lu'lu''s rise to power occurred. He had probably played a prominent role in the events leading to Mosul's loss of independence, and was well placed to profit from the opportunities with which he was soon presented.

His chance came when Arslān Shāh died, on Sunday night, 29 Rajab 607/16 January 1211.[10] Since he had long suffered from tuberculosis, his death was not unexpected, and he had planned for his succession. He intended that his two sons succeed him: the elder son ʿIzz al-Dīn Masʿūd was to rule Mosul; the younger, ʿImād al-Dīn Zankī, was to receive two fortresses in Kurdistan, al-ʿAqr and Shūsh. Arslān Shāh "ordered all the commanders of the army, amirs, notables, exemplars, ulama and the distinguished to take the oath"[11] accepting ʿIzz

8. Edhem, 95; Hennequin, 216, 218–22; al-Ḥusaynī, 50.

9. Abū Shāma, 76, citing the lost history of ʿIzz al-Dīn Ibn ʿAsākir (d. 643).

10. ʿIzz al-Dīn Ibn al-Athīr, *Ta'rīkh al-bāhir*, 197–98 (hereafter cited as *Bāhir*); *Kāmil*, 12:291; Ibn al-Sāʿī, *Muʿallim*, ff. 73b–74a; Sibṭ, 356; al-Mundhirī, 3:340; Abū Shāma, 70, 76; Ibn Khallikān, 1:193–94; Ibn al-ʿIbrī, 229; Bar Hebraeus, 1:366–67; Ibn Wāṣil, 3:202; Baybars al-Manṣūrī (Bodl.), ff. 79b–80a; al-Ṣafadī, *Al-Wāfī bi'l-wafayāt*, vol. 8, ed. Mohammed Youssef Najm, Bibliotheca Islamica, vol. 6h (Wiesbaden: Franz Steiner Verlag, 1391/1971), 750.

11. *Amara bi'akhdh al-mīthāq ʿalā kāffat al-awliyā' min al-ajnād wa'l-umarā' wa'l-aʿyān wa'l-amāthil wa'l-ʿulamā' wa'l-afāḍil* (*Bāhir*, 202).

al-Dīn Masʿūd as his successor. Since Masʿūd was still quite young,[12] Arslān Shāh

> wanted to strengthen him with one whom he made an advisor for him, a supporter to whom he could entrust the burden of the realm, to be an administrator[13] of his state and an overseer of its important affairs, and a deputy to him in the government of its subjects. So he examined his elite and his friends, his mamluks and his associates, his agents and his amirs, in order to select from among them one qualified for this great undertaking.[14]

Arslān Shāh chose the commander of his army (*Amīr al-Iṣfahsalār al-Kabīr*[15]), Badr al-Dīn Luʾluʾ, and promoted him gradually until "he entrusted him with the command of the army and the government of tribes and

12. Ibn al-Athīr says that Masʿūd was ten years old (*Kāmil*, 12:293; the word "ten" is placed in square brackets in the Tornberg edition). This is certainly an error, since his birth year is given as 590 by al-Mundhirī (4:321–2) and Ibn Khallikān (5:208). Ibn al-Athīr himself reports elsewhere that Masʿūd commanded Mosul's army in 606, and had a son aged ten when he died in 615. The corruption in the text of Ibn al-Athīr was apparently introduced quite early, however, for it is the most common age mentioned by later historians. See also al-Dhahabī, *ʿIbar*, 5:55; idem, *Taʾrīkh al-Islām*, Bibl. Nat. MS 1582, f. 221a; Ibn al-ʿImād al-Ḥanbalī, 5:62–63. Ibn Khaldūn (5, pt. 2, p. 594) reports al-Qāhir's age as 20. This is probably a publisher's or copyist's error, or an incorrect transcription by Ibn Khaldūn from Ibn al-Athīr.

13. On the title *mudabbir* see P. M. Holt, "The Structure of Government in the Mamluk Sultanate," in *The Eastern Mediterranean Lands in the Period of the Crusades*, ed. P. M. Holt (Warminster, England: Aris and Phillips, 1977), 54–55.

14. *Arāda an yashudd azrahu bi-man yajʿaluhu lahu wazīran, wa ʿalā mā fawwaḍa ilayhi min aʿbāʾ al-mamlaka ẓahīran, li-yakūna mudabbiran li-dawlatihi, wa nāẓiran fī mahāmm mamlakatihi, wa-nāʾiban ʿanhu fī wilāyat raʿīyatihi, faʿtabara khawāṣṣahu wa-awliyāʾahu, wa-mamālīkahu wa-aṣfiyāʾahu, wa-kufātahu wa-umarāʾahu, li-yakhtāra minhum man yakūnu ahlan li-hādhāʾl-amr al-kabīr* (*Bāhir*, 203).

15. *Bāhir*, 203. On the significance of this title, see C. E. Bosworth, "Ispahsālār," *EI2* 4 (1973):208–10; Humphreys, "Mamluk Army," 87–89.

clans."[16] Thus, at the time of Arslān Shāh's death, according to Ibn al-Athīr, Lu'lu' held a position of considerable power at court. Little else is known of Lu'lu''s origin and early career beyond Ibn al-Athīr's accolade. He was undoubtedly an Armenian from Rūm,[17] and some historians report that he had originally been owned by a tailor.[18] Of his career, all that is really known is that during Arslān Shāh's lifetime he was a mamluk amir[19] whose responsibilities included relaying important messages between the court and the Atabeg's trusted advisor Majd al-Dīn Ibn al-Athīr (brother of the historian, d. 606/1210).[20]

Arslān Shāh had died while on a boat returning to Mosul from 'Ayn al-Qayyāra, a mineral hot spring on the Tigris below Mosul, where he had sought relief from his illness. Lu'lu', who was accompanying him, concealed his death until he reached Mosul. He then ordered two mamluks to carry the body secretly into the palace, where he

16. *Wallāhu imārat al-juyūsh wa'l-'asākir wa-siyāsat al-qabā'il wa'l-'ashā'ir* (*Bāhir*, 204).

17. *Al-Ḥawādith*, 52; al-Dhahabī, *Ta'rīkh al-Islām*, Bodl. MS Laud 305, f. 305b; al-Yāfi'ī, 4:148. Al-Ruwayshidī (p. 27, n. 4) and al-Jalabī (p. 26) cite a source unavailable to me, the *Dīwān* of Ibn al-Muqarrab (d. 629).

18. Al-Birzālī, f. 430b; Ibn Kathīr, 13:214.

19. Yāqūt, *Mu'jam al-buldān*, 1:199–200; Ibn al-Sā'ī, *Jāmi'*, 299–300; idem, *Mu'allim*, ff. 73b, 78b; Ibn al-'Adīm, 3:187; Abū Shāma, 203; Ibn al-'Ibrī, 229; Bar Hebraeus, 1:367; Ibn Wāṣil, 3:202, 206; etc. Only Ibn al-Athīr (*Bāhir*, 198; *Kāmil*, 12:293) does not use the word *mamlūk*, employing instead the term *fatā*, meaning "young man." This word was probably chosen to dignify Lu'lu''s position, and perhaps to connote the type of virtuous young manhood (*futuwwa*) then being promoted by the caliph al-Nāṣir. This is an example of Ibn al-Athīr's delicacy concerning his patron's position.

20. Yāqūt, *The Irshád al-Aríb*, 6:238–41; Ibn al-Sā'ī, *Jāmi'*, 299–300.

ruled in Arslān Shāh's name until he was able to effect the orderly transfer of power to Arslān Shāh's sons. He sent 'Imād al-Dīn Ibn Yūnus, chief of Mosul's Shāfi'īs, to Baghdad to request recognition for the new rulers of Mosul and Kurdistan. The succession was promptly confirmed; Mas'ūd received the title al-Malik al-Qāhir and Zankī was named al-Malik al-Manṣūr.

Ibn al-Athīr's account of the succession[21] portrays Lu'lu' as the one individual selected and authorized by Arslān Shāh to preserve public order and guarantee the continuance of Zangid rule. There was, however, no obvious threat to al-Qāhir's succession, since al-'Ādil's strength and the Sinjār treaty of 606 virtually assured an orderly transfer of power. Ibn al-Athīr's account is overly dramatic and not in proportion to the uneventful nature of this episode. The effect of his presentation is to place Lu'lu' rather than al-Qāhir in Arslān Shāh's succession, and thereby provide his patron with a legitimate basis for his subsequent claim to authority.

Al-Qāhir's reign is not illuminated by surviving historical accounts. The tranquility of al-'Ādil's rule is partly responsible, but it seems also likely that Ibn al-Athīr did not wish to mention anything about the Zangid that would rival the heroic image he had established for Lu'lu'. The only report about Mosul reveals that its relations with Irbil were still good, for both cities contributed troops to an expedition undertaken by the Caliph to quell a rebellion in western Iran in

21. *Bāhir*, 201–4; *Kāmil*, 12:293–94. Other historians record no new details: see Ibn al-Sā'ī, *Mu'allim*, ff. 74b–75a, 76a, 78b–79a; Sibṭ, 356; Ibn al-'Ibrī, 229; Ibn Wāṣil, 3:202–6; Baybars al-Manṣūrī (Bodl.), ff. 79b–80a.

612/1215.[22] Ayyubid authority remained in effect in Mosul throughout al-Qāhir's reign, with al-'Ādil's name appearing on all issues of the city's coinage.[23] All that can be said of al-Qāhir himself is that he appears to have been popular with his subjects. When he died, on 27 Rabī' II 615/22 July 1218,[24] the people of Mosul manifested a degree of mourning unprecedented in the city's Atabegid history. According to Ibn al-Athīr's eye-witness account, the "people were stricken by his death; his loss was hard for them. He was loved by them and dear to their hearts. For his sake there was crying and wailing in every house."[25] Their grief may have been compounded by anxiety over the future of Mosul and the Zangid dynasty, for al-Qāhir's sons were too young to rule alone, and Lu'lu', as a mamluk, would not at that time have been an acceptable alternative.

22. *Kāmil*, 12:306; Juvaynī, *History of the World-Conquerer*, 2:702 (under year 611).

23. Issues of 607, 608, 609, 611, 612, and 614 are known. See Artuk, 410; Hennequin, 216–25; al-Ḥusaynī, 52, 115–16; Lane-Poole, 3:190–94; 9:304.

24. The date is uncertain. Ibn al-Athīr (*Kāmil*, 12:333) reports that al-Qāhir died on Monday night, three days remaining in Rabī' I, after a rule of seven years, nine months. However, this date is equivalent to 28 Rabī' I, or the night of Saturday–Sunday, 22–23 June; and the term of his rule would thus be only seven years, eight months. Ibn Khallikān (5:208) reports Monday night, three days remaining of Rabī' II, while al-Mundhirī (4:321–22) gives the date as dawn on the 27th of Rabī' II. The 27th was indeed a Monday, and accommodates a reign of the length specified by Ibn al-Athīr. Depending on whether the death occurred before or after midnight, the equivalent date could be Sunday or Monday, 22 or 23 July.

25. *Wa-uṣība ahlu bilādihi bi-mawtihi, wa-'aẓuma 'alayhim faqduhu, wa-kāna maḥbūban ilayhim, qarīban min qulūbihim, fa-fī kulli dārin li-ajlihi rannatun wa-'awīlun* (*Kāmil*, 12:334). An independent but similar eye-witness account is provided by Ibn al-Sā'ī, *Mu'allim*, f. 77a.

The Struggle over the Zangid Succession

Al-Qāhir had named his ten-year-old son Arslān Shāh his successor. Lu'lu' was to serve as his guardian (*waṣī*) and the administrator (*mudabbir*) of the state.[26] Lu'lu' quickly secured the loyalty of the army and the citizens of Mosul, and sent an envoy to Baghdad to obtain the Caliph's recognition. The Caliph is said to have recognized Lu'lu' himself as deputy sultan.[27] Lu'lu' then wrote to neighboring rulers to renew existing treaties on the same terms as had existed for al-Qāhir. From this point forward, Lu'lu' behaved as an independent ruler and used his own name on state correspondence.[28]

Lu'lu''s apparent usurpation of Zangid authority alarmed Arslān Shāh's uncle, ʿImād al-Dīn Zankī, who ruled the fortresses of al-ʿAqr and Shūsh and had expected to rule Mosul in the event of his brother's death. It is possible that his father had intended for him to rule if al-Qāhir should predecease him, for his position as the nearest adult relative of al-Qāhir gave him some claim to the throne in Saljuq and Zangid tradition.[29] But Zankī was at al-ʿAqr, and lacked the strength

26. The basic account of the succession is that of Ibn al-Athīr, *Kāmil*, 12:333–35. See also Ibn al-Sāʿī, *Muʿallim*, ff. 76a–77b; Ibn al-ʿIbrī, 231–32; Bar Hebraeus, 1:371–73; Ibn Wāṣil, 3:261–62; Baybars al-Manṣūrī (Bodl.), ff. 85b–86a.

27. Ibn al-Sāʿī, *Muʿallim*, f. 77b; cf. Ibn Khallikān, 1:194, where Lu'lu' is called *nāʾib*.

28. See Ḍiyāʾ al-Dīn Ibn al-Athīr (Bodl.), ff. 32b–34a, 38a–40a; (SOAS) ff. 39b–41a, 27a–29b.

29. There is some support for this theory in the titulature of the the later Zangids. The Caliph had granted Masʿūd the title al-Malik al-Qāhir and Zankī the title al-Malik al-Manṣūr, but no such title is known for Arslān Shāh. Perhaps Arslān Shāh's youth precluded his receiving such a title; but it may also be that Zankī was indeed intended to be Arslān Shāh's successor.

to press his claim on his own. Furthermore, it is unlikely that al-ʿĀdil would have permitted Mosul to be ruled by a vigorous legitimate successor to the Atabegid throne. Lu'lu' was left at peace to consolidate his position; he distributed largess to the people of Mosul, both rich and poor, thereby "changing their mourning clothes,"[30] and making them forget their sorrow at the death of al-Qāhir.

But just when Arslān Shāh's succession (under Lu'lu''s protection) might have seemed secure, al-ʿĀdil died, on 7 Jumādā II 615/31 August 1218. He was succeeded by his sons al-Kāmil, al-Muʿaẓẓam, and al-Ashraf, who were fully occupied for several years with threats posed by aggression from their Frankish and Saljuq enemies.[31] Taking advantage of the Ayyubids' preoccupation, many non-Ayyubid rulers sought ways to establish their independence or enlarge their territories.

Zankī clearly saw his chance to dislodge Lu'lu' from Mosul. He began by asking the garrison of al-ʿImādiya, the most important citadel in Kurdistan, to accept his authority, informing them that Arslān Shāh had died and that Lu'lu' had usurped the Zangid throne.[32] This story was readily believed because the young ruler was chronically ill and could rarely appear in public. The garrison submitted on 18 Ramaḍān 615/8 December 1218. Lu'lu' sent a force to recover it, but could not commit his full

30. *Wa-ghayyara thiyāba'l-ḥidād ʿanhum* (*Kāmil*, 12:334). Ibn al-Athīr's praise for Lu'lu' is expressed in terms very similar to those he employed for al-Qāhir in describing his succession to Arslān Shāh in the *Bāhir* (p. 202).

31. Gottschalk, *Al-Malik al-Kāmil*, 60–88; Humphreys, *Saladin*, 155–62.

32. His allegation may have been true. Ibn al-Athīr (*Kāmil*, 12:339) devotes only a few lines to Arslān Shāh's death and does not record an exact date or any details.

strength to the venture because Kūkburī of Irbil now began to support Zankī.[33] Lu'lu' attempted to convince Kūkburī to withdraw from the conflict; he wrote to rebuke him for his intervention into Mosul's internal affairs and remind him of his obligations under the treaty of 606, but his words were ignored. With Kūkburī threatening his flank, Lu'lu' was unable to concentrate his forces and his expedition at al-ʿImādiya was soon driven off. Other citadels of the al-Hakkāriya and al-Zawazān regions soon came to recognize Zankī's authority.

Lu'lu' required additional support to maintain his position against Zankī and Kūkburī. Since al-Ashraf was al-ʿĀdil's successor in the east and had just successfully staved off the invasion of the Rūm Saljuqs, it was to him that Lu'lu' turned for help. In exchange for his assistance, Lu'lu' acknowledged Mosul's subordination to al-Ashraf and al-Kāmil, the head of the Ayyubid confederation.[34] Al-Ashraf sent a warning to Kūkburī similar in tone to Lu'lu''s reprimand. He reminded him of his obligations under the treaty of 606, and demanded that the captured forts of Kurdistan be returned. Al-Ashraf threatened to invade his land if he refused. According to

33. Kūkburī's interference was warranted by his relationship to the Zangids, for he was the grandfather of Arslān Shāh and the father-in-law of Zankī. As such, it was expedient for him to protect the former and advance the claims of the latter. He could also claim to be supporting Ayyubid interests, since Arslān Shāh's mother and Zankī's wife were both daughters of Rabīʿa Khātūn, the sister of Ṣalāḥ al-Dīn and al-ʿĀdil, who had long been Kūkburī's wife. On Zankī's challenge to Lu'lu' see: *Kāmil*, 12:335–37; Ibn al-Sāʿī, *Muʿallim*, ff. 77b, 79a; Ibn Wāṣil, 4:20–22.

34. Coins of 615 are known bearing the names of al-Ashraf, al-Kāmil and Arslān Shāh. See al-Ḥusaynī, 53. Lu'lu''s overtures to al-Ashraf are described by Ibn al-Athīr, *Kāmil*, 12:337–38; Ibn al-Sāʿī, *Muʿallim*, ff. 77b, 79b; Ibn al-ʿIbrī, 232; and Ibn Wāṣil, 4:22.

Ibn al-Athīr, al-Ashraf accused Kūkburī of hindering the Muslim effort to drive the Franks of the Fifth Crusade from Egypt.[35] Kūkburī ignored the Ayyubid's threat and countered with one of his own: he allied with the Artuqid rulers of Mārdīn and Ḥiṣn Kayfā against al-Ashraf. Al-Ashraf responded by sending a small force to Naṣībīn, where it would be able either to aid Lu'lu' or deflect an Artuqid offensive.

Zankī and Kūkburī continued to raid Mosul's territory. Forces sent by Lu'lu' to defend his border attacked and defeated Zankī near al-ʿAqr on Sunday, 27 Muḥarram 616/14 April 1219.[36] Lu'lu' announced his victory to the Caliph in a letter drafted by Ḍiyā' al-Dīn Ibn al-Athīr.[37] Ḍiyā' al-Dīn affirmed Lu'lu''s loyalty to the Caliph and charged that Zankī's aggression was illegal. He argued that Lu'lu' was innocent of starting the conflict since his troops had attacked entirely on their own initiative. He also declared that Lu'lu' would accept whatever terms the Caliph might impose, but that Zankī too must be content to accept them. Envoys of al-Ashraf and the Caliph then visited Lu'lu' and Kūkburī to witness their oaths to keep peace. Since each ruler was permitted

35. *Kāmil*, 12:337–38. The responsibility of Muslim rulers to devote their energies to the holy war rather than fight one another was one of Ibn al-Athīr's favorite themes. While al-Ashraf was undoubtedly concerned with the Crusader threat, his primary interest was in maintaining his power in northern Syria in the face of the many external and internal threats arising upon the death of al-ʿĀdil. See Emmanuel Sivan, *L'Islam et la Croisade, idéologie et propagande dans les réactions musulmanes aux Croisades* (Paris: Librairie d'Amérique et d'Orient, 1968), 43–50.

36. On this battle, see *Kāmil*, 12:338; Ibn al-Sāʿī, *Muʿallim*, ff. 79b–80a; Bar Hebraeus, 1:373–74; Ibn Wāṣil, 4:24–25.

37. Ḍiyā' al-Dīn Ibn al-Athīr (Bodl.), ff. 32b–34a; (SOAS), ff. 39b–41a. Cf. Margoliouth, 13.

to keep the territories he controlled, it seems that the Caliph considered Zankī's position equal to Arslān Shāh's. But the peace was short-lived. Arslān Shāh died shortly thereafter, and his three-year-old brother Nāṣir al-Dīn Maḥmūd was placed on the throne by Lu'lu'. Kūkburī and Zankī immediately launched new attacks on Mosul.[38]

Arslān Shāh's death left Lu'lu' in a weaker position than ever. Mosul's army was in Syria supporting Ayyubid activities there,[39] so Lu'lu' was forced to call upon al-Ashraf's garrison in Naṣībīn for help against Kūkburī and Zankī. When the reinforcements arrived, Lu'lu' set out to engage the enemy. The battle, which took place on 20 Rajab 616/1 October 1219, was inconclusive. The Ayyubid wing of Mosul's army defeated Zankī, while Lu'lu''s wing was defeated by Kūkburī. Ibn al-Athīr, who is the sole authority for this event, is careful to mention several circumstances which excuse Lu'lu''s defeat, but his efforts cannot entirely conceal his patron's deteriorating position.[40]

Lu'lu''s survival did nothing to increase his security. Although envoys sent by the Caliph established a truce that allowed each side to keep what territories it controlled, Lu'lu''s authority continued to shrink. The garrison of the citadel of Kawāshā, the last of Lu'lu''s

38. The new struggle with Zankī is described by Ibn al-Athīr, *Kāmil*, 12:339–41. Other accounts, all similar to Ibn al-Athīr's, are Ibn al-Sā'ī, *Mu'allim*, ff. 77b–78a; Ibn al-'Ibrī, 232–33; Bar Hebraeus, 1:374–75; Ibn Wāṣil, 4:25–28.

39. Al-Ashraf attacked a Crusader fort in northern Syria. See Gottschalk, *Al-Malik al-Kāmil*, 97.

40. Gottschalk (*Al-Malik al-Kāmil*, 96–98) provides a detailed account of the battle. My forthcoming article in *Studia Islamica* contains an analysis of Ibn al-Athīr's treatment of the battle.

strongholds in Kurdistan, now openly declared its support for Zankī.[41] Lu'lu''s position appears to have been on the verge of collapse. The defeat of his army by Zankī and Kūkburī, the loss of Kurdistan, the lack of any legitimate basis for his authority following the death of Arslān Shāh II—all worked to make Mosul a most attractive target for absorption by Irbil or the Ayyubids. Lu'lu' was saved only by the eruption of a rebellion in the Ayyubid army, which gave him the opportunity to prove his usefulness to them in a way perhaps unforeseen by anyone.

The Kurdish Revolt and the Suppression of the Zangids

In a final effort to prevent his collapse, Lu'lu' invited al-Ashraf to come to Mosul to shore up his authority.[42] Al-Ashraf prepared an army in Shaʿbān 616/October–November 1219 and wintered at Ḥarrān. Kūkburī renewed his alliance with the Artuqid rulers of Ḥiṣn Kayfā and Mārdīn, and further strengthened his position by recognizing the authority of ʿIzz al-Dīn Kaykāwus, the powerful ruler of Rūm, who had recently fought al-Ashraf for the possession of territory near Aleppo. Kūkburī also sought support within the Ayyubid army, where Kurdish troops were growing increasingly resentful of their treatment and status in relation to the rising prestige of mamluk and Turkman units. Two prominent Kurdish amirs, ʿImād al-Dīn Ibn al-Mashṭūb and ʿIzz al-Dīn Ibn Badr

41. *Kāmil*, 12:341; Ibn al-Sāʿī, *Muʿallim*, f. 80b; Ibn al-ʿIbrī, 233, Bar Hebraeus, 1:375; Ibn Wāṣil, 4:31.

42. Al-Ashraf's advance toward Mosul and Kūkburī's response: *Kāmil*, 12:341–42; Ibn al-Sāʿī, *Muʿallim*, f. 80b; Ibn al-ʿAdīm, 3:188; Bar Hebraeus, 1:375; Ibn Wāṣil, 4:30–31.

al-Ḥumaydī, responded to his call and lead their followers in revolt.[43]

The two amirs withdrew from al-Ashraf's camp and stood in his path toward Mosul. Al-Ashraf was able to disperse them with little difficulty, and Ibn al-Mashṭūb was captured by the Zangid ruler of Sinjār[44] in the course of his flight toward Irbil. The ruler of Sinjār was evidently attracted by the merits of a Zangid-Kurdish alliance, for he soon released Ibn al-Mashṭūb and joined the revolt. The rebels then occupied a fort called Tall Ya'far on Sinjār's border with Mosul and raided the adjacent territory. Lu'lu' and al-Ashraf's Naṣībīn garrison besieged Ibn al-Mashṭūb in Tall Ya'far for a month and captured it on 17 Rabī' II 617/21 June 1220.[45] Lu'lu' promised Ibn al-Mashṭūb safe-conduct in exchange for the surrender of the fort and took him to Mosul. The rebel received a warm welcome from the people of the city, suggesting that the Kurdish cause he represented had

43. Gottschalk, *Al-Malik al-Kāmil*, 98–101; Humphreys, *Saladin*, 94, 117, 122, 162–63; Ayalon, "Aspects," 54:8–10, 22. The primary sources for Ibn al-Mashṭūb are *Kāmil*, 12:342–43; Sibṭ, 400; Ibn al-'Adīm, 3:187–89; Ibn Khallikān, 1:180–84; Bar Hebraeus, 1:375–77; Ibn Wāṣil, 4:28–30, 70–73, 76–77.

44. His name is uncertain. Ibn al-Athīr calls him 'Umar b. Muḥammad (*Kāmil*, 12:355) and Farrūkh Shāh b. Zankī (12:342). Ibn Wāṣil speaks of Farrūkh Shāh Maḥmūd b. Muḥammad (4:71–72), Maḥmūd Farrūkh Shāh (4:73), Maḥmūd (4:74), and al-Malik al-Amjad Maḥmūd (4:105). Since Arslān Shāh II of Mosul was known as 'Alī before the death of his grandfather Arslān Shāh I (Abū Shāma, 114; Ibn Khallikān, 5:208), it is possible that both Maḥmūd and 'Umar are correct. Concerning the name Farrūkh Shāh, it seems that the later Zangids of Sinjār may have come to adopt names ending in "Shāh" as a title. Farrūkh Shāh's brother, 'Abd al-Raḥman (d. 651), for example, was also known as Sulṭān Shāh; see al-Ghassānī, 597.

45. *Kāmil*, 12:343.

considerable popularity there.[46] Lu'lu', however, soon handed him over to al-Ashraf, who imprisoned him at Ḥarrān, where he died two years later.

Once al-Ashraf had gained control of his army, he continued his advance toward Mosul, determined to suppress the Zangids before they could incite further rebellion in his army. At Naṣībīn he learned that the ruler of Sinjār was prepared to give him his city in exchange for al-Raqqa, a town on the Euphrates.[47] The ruler of Sinjār was insecure on his throne, for he had come to power by assassinating his brother ('Imād al-Dīn Shāhanshāh) and he feared the same fate at the hands of his advisors. The loss of the fort Tall Ya'far to Lu'lu' had further weakened his position. Al-Ashraf readily accepted his offer; ninety-three years of Zangid rule in Sinjār ended at the beginning of Jumādā I 617/July 1220.

Al-Ashraf proceeded to Mosul, arriving on Tuesday, 19 Jumādā I 617/22 July 1220.[48] Negotiations were begun to resolve the conflict between Mosul and Irbil. A compromise was proposed that all the forts captured from Lu'lu' were to be returned, except for al-'Imādiya. Al-Ashraf demanded in addition that Kūkburī recognize his authority on coinage and in the *khuṭba*. Kūkburī rejected the proposals, prolonging discussions for two months. Finally al-Ashraf grew tired of remaining in the field and

46. Only Ibn Wāṣil (4:72) records this detail.

47. Cession of Sinjār to al-Ashraf: *Kāmil*, 12:343–44; Ibn al-Sā'ī, *Mu'allim*, ff. 80b–81a; Sibṭ, 401; Ibn al-'Adīm, 3:189; Ibn Shaddād, *A'lāq*, f. 35a; Bar Hebraeus, 1:377; Ibn Wāṣil, 4:73–74; Ibn al-Fuwaṭī, *Talkhīṣ*, 4:693–94.

48. The date may be incorrect, for the 22 July was a Wednesday. On al-Ashraf's stay in Mosul and the truce negotiations: *Kāmil*, 12:344–45; Ibn al-Sā'ī, *Mu'allim*, f. 81a; Ibn al-'Adīm, 3:189–90; Bar Hebraeus, 1:377–78; Ibn al-'Ibrī, 233; Ibn Wāṣil, 4:75–76; *Ḥawādith*, 105.

marched toward Irbil to force Kūkburī to accept terms. Kūkburī at last agreed and a truce was concluded in Sha'bān 617/October 1220. Kūkburī put Zankī in al-Ashraf's custody to ensure that the captured forts surrendered as agreed. Zankī's inherited territories, al-'Aqr and Shūsh, were to be turned over to agents of al-Ashraf, who would keep them for Zankī until he was released. But before the agreement could be fully implemented, envoys from al-Kāmil in Egypt arrived. They reported that the Egyptian city of Dimyāṭ had been lost to the Fifth Crusade, and al-Ashraf's army was urgently needed to defend the country from further loss. Al-Ashraf left Mosul on 2 Ramaḍān 617/31 October 1220 and took Zankī with him.

Kūkburī never acknowledged al-Ashraf's supremacy, although he accepted al-Kāmil;[49] and even though the forts in Kurdistan nearly all refused to surrender, Zankī soon obtained his freedom through the mediation of al-Ashraf's brother Shihāb al-Dīn Ghāzī. Only Lu'lu' was forced to sacrifice appreciable territory, for al-Ashraf demanded of him Tall Ya'far, the fort he had captured from Ibn al-Mashṭūb. Nonetheless, the truce established Lu'lu''s authority as the guardian of a Zangid succession firmly subordinate to the Ayyubids.

The Foundations of Lu'lu''s Independent Rule

Despite the incomplete implementation of the truce between Mosul and Irbil, Lu'lu''s position had been effectively secured by the events of 617. Al-Ashraf had not seen fit to negotiate directly with Zankī, thereby implying that he deserved no more consideration than a rebellious vassal like Ibn al-Mashṭūb. Zankī's weakness was

49. See Artuk, 410–11; Edhem, 102, 141; Hennequin, 226–28; al-Ḥusaynī, 70–71; Lane-Poole, 3:197; 9:311.

further revealed by Kūkburī's willingness to give him to al-Ashraf as a hostage. His authority eroded to the point that the garrisons of his forts refused to obtain his release by submitting to al-Ashraf's agents. Lu'lu''s position was correspondingly strengthened, for the truce clearly upheld his right to rule the Kurdish forts, although it would be up to him to occupy them.

Lu'lu''s power grew under al-Ashraf's protection. The Kurdish groups and garrisons, previously loyal to Zankī, gradually came to accept his authority.[50] In Muḥarram 618/February–March 1221, the garrisons of the forts of al-Hakkāriya and al-Zawazān wrote to ask his forgiveness. Al-ʿImādiya also went over to Lu'lu', even though the treaty had assigned it to Zankī. As a dependent of al-Ashraf, Lu'lu' had to ask his permission to assume control of the forts. Al-Ashraf at first refused, but finally yielded when Lu'lu' agreed to transfer to him a fort and some lands near Naṣībīn. Mosul and Irbil were sufficiently reconciled that both contributed troops to an expedition, organized by the Caliph and commanded by Kūkburī, to ward off a Mongol raiding party in Ṣafar 618/March–April 1221.[51]

Al-Ashraf's journey to Egypt kept him away from the Jazīra for about a year. In the fall of 618/1221 he came to al-Raqqa and deposed its Zangid ruler (the former ruler of Sinjār).[52] He spent some time at al-Raqqa and

50. *Kāmil*, 12:346–47; Bar Hebraeus, 1:378–79. According to Ibn al-Sāʿī (*Muʿallim*, f. 81b), Lu'lu' solicited their return.

51. *Kāmil*, 12:377–79; Ibn Bībī, 114–16; Ibn Wāṣil, 4:49–51. Chingiz Khan had sent part of his army, under the generals Jebe and Sübedei, to capture the Khwārazm Shāh Muḥammad. They invaded Adharbayjān and approached Irbil in the course of their pursuit. See Boyle, "Dynastic and Political History of the Īl-Khāns," 310–11; Grousset, 245–47.

52. Ibn Wāṣil, 4:105. The Zangid died soon after he was dispossessed. He had three brothers, Sayf al-Dīn Zankī, Muẓaffar al-Dīn Mūsā

then returned to Egypt at the beginning of 619/February–March 1222. Lu'lu' continued to press Zankī and besieged and captured Shūsh, one of the mountain fortresses that Zankī had received as his inheritance.[53] Zankī had left his territories to go to Adharbayjān to lend aid to Uzbak Ibn Pahlawān, who was extending his domains in the political vacuum created by the departure of the Mongols.[54] According to Ibn al-Sā'ī, Zankī came back to Kurdistan and recaptured Shūsh, but was then compelled by Kūkburī to exchange both al-'Aqr and Shūsh for distant Shahrazūr.[55] By placing Zankī in Shahrazūr, more than a hundred miles from Mosul, Kūkburī showed his determination to control both Zankī and the issue of the Zangid succession in Mosul.

Lu'lu''s security, however, was soon threatened from another quarter. The collapse of the Fifth Crusade freed the Ayyubids from external threats for the first time in five years. As they turned their full attention to internal affairs, a succession conflict over the throne of Ḥamāh pitted al-Mu'aẓẓam of Damascus against his brothers al-Kāmil and al-Ashraf.[56] A three-phase civil war broke out, each phase involving a wider circle of participants.

(d. 645), and Sulṭān Shāh 'Abd al-Raḥman (d. 651). It is known of the latter two that they moved to Baghdad and joined the service of the Caliph. See Sibṭ, 399–400; Abū Shāma, 120; Ibn al-Fuwaṭī, *Talkhīṣ*, 4:693–4; and al-Ghassānī, 597.

53. *Kāmil*, 12:411–12; Ibn al-Sā'ī, *Mu'allim*, ff. 81b–82a; Ibn Wāṣil, 4:114–15; al-Dhahabī, *Ta'rīkh al-Islām*, Br. Libr., f. 195a.

54. Uzbak had survived the Mongol occupation by paying a substantial tribute. See Grousset, 245, 260. Zankī probably hoped to find in him a new ally capable of furthering his claim to the throne of Mosul.

55. Ibn al-Sā'ī, *Mu'allim*, f. 82b; See also Ibn Khallikān, 5:208.

56. Gottschalk, *Al-Malik al-Kāmil*, 116–20; Humphreys, *Saladin*, 170–73.

Initially, al-Muʿaẓẓam acted alone; he invaded Ḥamāh in 620/1223, but was forced to withdraw when al-Ashraf and al-Kāmil threatened to attack him. He then sought broader support and encouraged al-Ashraf's brother, Shihāb al-Dīn Ghāzī, to revolt in Armenia. He also won the support of Kūkburī, who undoubtedly remained dissatisfied with al-Ashraf's resolution of the Zangid succession. Al-Kāmil and al-Ashraf commanded troops from Mosul, Aleppo, Ḥamāh, and Ḥimṣ. They won further support from Kayqubādh of Rūm, whose name joins theirs on Mosul's coins of 620 and 621.[57]

The second phase of the war began in the summer of 621/1224 and also resulted in victory for al-Ashraf and al-Kāmil.[58] Ghāzī was easily defeated by al-Ashraf, and al-Muʿaẓẓam could not conquer Ḥamāh because of al-Kāmil's threatening presence in Egypt. Kūkburī besieged Mosul for ten days in Jumādā II 621/July 1224, but withdrew to Irbil when he heard of Ghāzī's defeat and the approach of a force sent by al-Ashraf to relieve Mosul. Although al-Muʿaẓẓam had again been defeated, he was no weaker than before and continued his attempts to strengthen his position. When the Khwārazm Shāh Jalāl al-Dīn arrived in Iraq in the winter of 621/1224–25, al-Muʿaẓẓam recognized an unparalleled opportunity to tip the balance of power in his favor.

Jalāl al-Dīn had established himself in western Iran following the withdrawal of the Mongol invaders who had

57. Edhem, 98–99; al-Ḥusaynī, 55. The validity of reading Kayqubādh's name on these coins is questioned by Hennequin, 228–29.

58. Gottschalk, *Al-Malik al-Kāmil*, 121–26; Humphreys, *Saladin*, 173–76. Mosul's involvement is detailed in *Kāmil*, 12:421–4; Ibn Naẓīf, ff. 148a–b (Doudou's translation of this passage, 70–71, is misleading); Sibṭ, 416–17; Ibn al-ʿAdīm, 3:195–96; Abū Shāma, 133–34, 142; Ibn Wāṣil, 4:137–42.

destroyed his father's kingdom.[59] He then made a devastating foray through the Caliph's territory in Khūzistān and Iraq, and camped at the village of Daqūqā, north of Baghdad, until the end of Rabīʿ I 622/April 1225.[60] There he received various envoys sent by the rulers of the region to try to define their relations to this new force in Iraq. Kūkburī was among those who sent presents and offered his submission. ʿImād al-Dīn Zankī of Shahrazūr promised Mosul to Jalāl al-Dīn, probably in the hope that the Shāh could be induced to capture the city and allow Zankī to rule it under his protection. It is surely no coincidence that a dinar minted in Zankī's name is dated to this year, and that it gives Zankī the title Atabeg.[61]

Lu'lu' was justifiably anxious about the presence of Jalāl al-Dīn in the area, for the Khwārazm Shāh's intentions were openly hostile and his troops had raided into Mosul's territory. Letters written by Ḍiyā' al-Dīn Ibn al-Athīr to the Caliph on Lu'lu''s behalf contain apologies for not sending forces to help fight Jalāl al-Dīn, but otherwise support the Caliph's position toward the Khwārazm Shāh.[62] Nothing came of Jalāl al-Dīn's invasion of Iraq, but he had made an impressive show of strength.

59. On the Khwārazm Shāh and his rule in Western Iran, see Boyle, "Dynastic and Political History of the Īl-Khāns," 322–29; Gottschalk, *Al-Malik al-Kāmil*, 126–28; Humphreys, *Saladin*, 176–78.

60. On Jalāl al-Dīn in Iraq: Ibn Naẓīf, ff. 149b–50a; Juvaynī, 2:422–24; Bar Hebraeus, 1:394; Ibn Wāṣil, 4:143–46. Juvaynī states that Jalāl al-Dīn defeated Kūkburī in battle, but this is not mentioned by the others.

61. Al-Ḥusaynī, 68. Only the Zangid rulers of Mosul used this title on their coins. As such, its use by Zankī must represent his claim to be ruler of Mosul. The coin names Kūkburī, rather than Jalāl al-Dīn, as Zankī's overlord. Other coins of the Shahrazūr Zangids are described in Hennequin, 359–60.

62. Margoliouth, 15–16.

When he returned to Iran and defeated the Georgians, his ascendancy became so evident that al-Muʿaẓẓam invited him to join the alliance against al-Ashraf and al-Kāmil.

The final phase of the Ayyubid civil war[63] began in 623/1226 with al-Muʿaẓẓam's position stronger than ever. He had rendered al-Kāmil harmless by fostering disunity in the Egyptian army; only the outbreak of an epidemic among his horses prevented him from capturing Ḥamāh. Kūkburī's role was merely to threaten Mosul and prevent Lu'lu' from aiding al-Ashraf, which he accomplished by camping on the Zab River, his border with Mosul, in Jumādā II 623/June 1226. There were no hostilities, but the threat was sufficient to keep Mosul out of the war.[64] Al-Ashraf experienced the worst of the fighting. Not only did Jalāl al-Dīn invade Armenia, but both Artuqid rulers revolted. Al-Ashraf was unable to cope with these catastrophes alone, and called upon his ally Kayqubādh of Rūm to help him deal with the Artuqids. Kayqubādh conducted a successful campaign, but then quarreled with

63. Boyle, "Dynastic and Political History of the Īl-Khāns," 328–29; Gottschalk, *Al-Malik al-Kāmil*, 132–37; Humphreys, *Saladin*, 178–81. For the role of Mosul and its neighbors, see *Kāmil*, 12:453–54; Ibn Naẓīf, ff. 154b–55a; Ibn Wāṣil, 4:176–77, 187–89.

64. Kūkburī's participation in this action undoubtedly created great hardship for both Mosul and Irbil. The winter of 622/1225 had been very cold and there had been much more rain and snow than usual (*Kāmil*, 12:443–44, 447–49, 466–67). Food became scarce and prices rose excessively, leading to famine. The weakened population fell victim to a severe epidemic (*wabāʾ*), whose effects did not spare the upper classes. Of thirty-three ulama known to be resident in the city, more than one quarter died (see Patton, "History of the Atabegs," 164, 353). Obviously, such a heavy death toll among the ulama indicates an even heavier rate among the majority of the population. The disaster did not soon abate. Weather continued to be poor throughout 623, with no rain at all in the spring, and the few crops that did survive were eaten by locusts.

al-Ashraf over the control of the territory his armies had occupied. The two armies fought in Shawwāl 623/October 1226 and al-Ashraf's army was defeated.

The involvement of both Jalāl al-Dīn and Kayqubādh in the Ayyubid conflict forced al-Ashraf to attempt a reconciliation with al-Muʿaẓẓam. He entered Damascus in Shawwāl 623/September 1226 and spent nine months there in semi-captivity. The histories record several diplomatic efforts during this time, as Lu'lu' and other regional rulers attempted to learn the significance of al-Ashraf's stay in Damascus and redefine their relations with each other in light of it.[65] Al-Ashraf eventually promised his support for al-Muʿaẓẓam and was released, but as soon as he was out of Damascus he repudiated his word.[66] The Ayyubids appeared to be faced with another round of the civil war, but before it could begin al-Muʿaẓẓam died, on Friday, 1 Dhu'l-Ḥijja 624/12 November 1227. Al-Kāmil was left as the leading ruler of the Ayyubid confederation. The major focus of his rule was to be the problem of unifying the various Ayyubid states under his authority.[67] This reorientation of Ayyubid priorities afforded Lu'lu' the chance to extend his control over Mosul and establish himself as an independent ruler.

Lu'lu''s authority had grown gradually since al-Ashraf had ended the Zangid threat. His earliest efforts had been directed toward consolidating his control over Kurdistan in the wake of the Zangids' suppression. In 619/1222 he had undertaken his first independent military operation there, capturing the citadel of Shūsh

65. Ibn Naẓīf, ff. 158a–b. See also Humphreys, *Saladin*, 182–83; Gottschalk, *Al-Malik al-Kāmil*, 137–44.

66. Gottschalk, *Al-Malik al-Kāmil*, 140; Humphreys, *Saladin*, 182–83.

67. Gottschalk, *Al-Malik al-Kāmil*, 146–52, 161–67; Humphreys, *Saladin*, 170, 185, 197–207, 214–15, 442–43 (n. 27).

from ʿImād al-Dīn Zankī. This was followed by a greater display of force when the garrison of the citadel of al-ʿImādiya revolted in 622/1225.[68] The rebels wrote to Zankī, Kūkburī, and Shihāb al-Dīn Ghāzī, offering submission to each, but received no active support. Lu'lu' sent a force to besiege them under the command of his son Amīn al-Dīn. In Dhu'l-Qaʿda 622/November 1225 Lu'lu' reached a surrender agreement with the leaders of the rebel party, and envoys came to Mosul to swear an oath to abide by its terms. The rebels did not all agree, however, and the dissenters turned the fort over to Amīn al-Dīn while the envoys were in Mosul. The capture of Shūsh and al-ʿImādiya are the first signs of Lu'lu''s growing strength and ability.

As Ayyubid influence over the Jazīra waned, both Mosul and Irbil fostered their relations with Baghdad. During al-Ashraf's captivity in Damascus Lu'lu' undertook independent negotiations with Kūkburī and the Caliph concerning a civil problem in Kurdistan.[69] In 625/1227–28 Lu'lu' engaged a daughter to ʿAlā' al-Dīn Abū Shujāʿ Alṭibars, known as al-Duwaydār al-Kabīr (d. 650), one of al-Mustanṣir's leading mamluks. The wealth of the groom and the value of the marriage may be estimated from the bride price of twenty thousand dinars, in addition to gifts of gold, silver, and clothing.[70] In return, the Caliph used his influence to protect his new friends. When the Khwārazm Shāh invaded Armenia in 629/1229 and besieged Khilāṭ, the Caliph sent him an envoy to ask that he not interfere with Lu'lu' and Kūkburī.[71]

68. *Kāmil*, 12:444–46.
69. Ibn Naẓīf, f. 158b.
70. Ibn Naẓīf, f. 173a; Ibn al-Fuwaṭī, *Talkhīṣ*, 2:850; al-Dhahabī, *Ta'rīkh al-Islām*, Bodl. MS Laud 305, ff. 6b, 237b; al-Ghassānī, 590–92.
71. Al-Nasawī, 304.

But Lu'lu' was surpassed by Kūkburī in his desire to cultivate the favor of the Caliph. In Muḥarram 628/November 1230, Kūkburī visited Baghdad and named the Caliph his successor in Irbil.[72] His magnanimous gesture was undoubtedly motivated by both his rivalry with Lu'lu' and his anxiety at the reappearance of the Mongol army in Iran. He had good reason to fear the Mongols. In the winter of 628/1231 they defeated Jalāl al-Dīn and dispersed his armies; they then looted throughout the regions of Naṣībīn, Sinjār, the Khābūr, and 'Arābān while pursuing the scattering Khwārazmians. At the same time another Mongol party advanced from Adharbayjān into Iraq and raided in the vicinity of Irbil. Another raid into Iraq was launched the following spring.[73]

The Caliph and Kūkburī combined their armies and spent the spring and summer of 629/1232 shadowing the Mongols without, however, meeting them in open battle.[74] Kūkburī, who was nearly eighty years old, grew ill on this campaign and returned to Irbil, where he soon died, on Friday, 14 Ramaḍān 630/24 June 1233. The Caliph occupied Irbil, overcoming a brief resistance by some of Kūkburī's followers.[75] They had sought support from the Ayyubids and from Zankī in Shahrazūr to no avail, and the city fell to the Caliph's forces on 17 Shawwāl/27 July

72. Sibṭ, 450; Ibn Wāṣil, 5:50; *Ḥawādith*, 19–23; al-Yūnīnī, 1:111; al-Dhahabī, *Ta'rīkh al-Islām*, Bodl. MS Laud 305, f. 9a; Ibn Kathīr, 13:129.

73. *Kāmil*, 12:497–504; Ibn Naẓīf, ff. 210a–b.

74. Ibn Naẓīf, f. 212a; Bar Hebraeus, 1:396–97; *Ḥawādith*, 27–31; al-Dhahabī, *Ta'rīkh al-Islām*, Bodl. MS Laud 305, ff. 9a–b.

75. Ibn Naẓīf, f. 223a; Sibṭ, 450; al-Makīn Ibn al-'Amīd, 140; Ibn Khallikān, 4:113–21; Ibn al-'Ibrī, 249; Bar Hebraeus, 1:399; Ibn Wāṣil, 5:48–62; *Ḥawādith*, 44–50; Ibn al-Ṭiqṭaqā, 41–42; al-Dhahabī, *Ta'rīkh al-Islām*, Bodl. MS Laud 305, f. 10a; Ibn Kathīr, 13:135; al-Ghassānī, 452–55.

1233. The mamluk Shams al-Dīn Bātkīn al-Rūmī, previously the Caliph's governor in Basra, was made governor of Irbil.[76]

Kūkburī's death removed the last obstacle to Lu'lu''s independent rule in Mosul. So long as Kūkburī harbored a rival claimant to the Zangid throne and enjoyed the protection of the Caliph, Lu'lu' had to maintain the fiction of Zangid rule in Mosul. With Kūkburī dead and the Caliph in possession of Irbil, Lu'lu' was able to advance his position in Mosul without fear of reprisal. No other ruler had any interest in preserving Zangid rule. In 631, the Atabeg Nāṣir al-Dīn Maḥmūd simply disappeared,[77] probably executed by Lu'lu'. Lu'lu' petitioned the Caliph to recognize his independent rule in Mosul. His request was granted, and in Rabīʿ I 631/December 1233, Lu'lu' was invested as sultan by the Caliph's envoy. He received the title al-Malik al-Raḥīm, and was authorized to place his name in the *khuṭba* and on Mosul's coins.[78] One hundred six years of Zangid rule over Mosul had ended.

76. Ibn Khallikān, 3:504; *Ḥawādith*, 180–83; al-Ṣafadī, 10:66–67.

77. Ibn al-Sāʿī, *Muʿallim*, f. 78b. My arguments for placing Lu'lu''s usurpation of the Zangid dynasty in this year are stated in "Ibn al-Sāʿī's Account," 153–157. Other accounts of Lu'lu''s succession are: Ibn Naẓīf, f. 226b; Sibṭ, 417; Abū Shāma, 114, 142; Ibn Khallikān, 1:194; Ibn al-ʿIbrī, 249; Bar Hebraeus, 1:399–400; Ibn Wāṣil, 4:114–5; 5:50; *Ḥawādith*, 52; al-Birzālī, ff. 412b–13a; al-Dhahabī, *ʿIbar* 5:81; idem, *Ta'rīkh al-Islām*, Bodl. MS Laud 305, ff. 10b, 305b; Ibn Kathīr, 13:136; al-Ghassānī, 457.

78. Other accounts of the investiture are in Ibn Naẓīf, f. 226b; Ibn al-ʿIbrī, 249; *Ḥawādith*, 52; al-Dhahabī, *Ta'rīkh al-Islām*, Bodl. MS Laud 305, f. 10b; al-Ghassānī, 457. Some of Mosul's coins for 631 bear the name of Maḥmūd, but the majority proclaim Lu'lu'. See Artuq, 415; Edhem, 101, 110; Hennequin, 234–35; al-Ḥusaynī, 119–120; Krehl, 256–58; Lane-Poole, 3:199, 202–3; 9:306.

2
The Years of Independent Rule

Lu'lu''s security as the independent ruler of Mosul was now assured. The remaining twenty-six years of his reign were occupied in unceasing efforts to expand his realm and maintain his independence. Unfortunately it is difficult to construct a coherent picture of his activities during this time, primarily because after the death of Ibn al-Athīr in 630/1233 Mosul was left with no historian to record its perspective. Mosul's role in history must be reconstructed from passing references in works written by authors in other cities, which naturally reflect the outlook of their patrons and stress the events of local interest. Three distinct perspectives survive, representing the interests of Ayyubid, Mamluk, and Mongol era historians. The difficulties of the period are manifested especially in the scarcity of detail, rendering basic facts and chronology difficult to establish, and in the absence of commentary on Lu'lu''s policies and motivation.

Nevertheless, the historical record is complete enough to reveal the broad outlines of Lu'lu''s relations with the Ayyubids, the Caliph, and the Mongols. It is clear that he was determined to expand his territories in the Jazīra, toward which end he involved himself in the rivalries among the Ayyubid rulers and cultivated close relations with the Caliph al-Mustanṣir. As Mongol power in the region grew and their direct conflict with the Ayyubids and the Caliph became imminent, Lu'lu' moved gradually from a position of intermediary between the Mongols and Ayyubids to one of direct subordination. His conduct won him favored status with the Mongols. When the Mongols began their invasion of Iraq, Lu'lu' aided them and attempted to exploit their power to acquire further territory. After Lu'lu''s death, his sons fled to Egypt and participated in a disastrous effort, sponsored by Sultan Baybars, to extend mamluk authority into Iraq. The result was a resounding defeat for the "sons of the Lord of Mosul" and the destruction of Mosul by the Mongols.

While a fairly reliable history of Mosul's involvement in regional affairs can be presented, one can only speculate about underlying factors. Lu'lu''s efforts to expand Mosul's domain over the Jazīra may have resulted from a desire to exploit Ayyubid weakness and disunity, to establish independence, or to secure the region from Khwārazmian domination. His relations with the Caliph may have been motivated by the need for political support against the Ayyubids, the Zangids, the Mongols, or by a desire to keep the good opinion of the ulama in Mosul itself. Lu'lu''s submission to the Mongols may have been furthered by either greed or fear, if not both, depending on how their presence affected him. The absence of any local historian to explain, defend, or even allude to the policy underlying Lu'lu''s actions is a serious loss to our understanding of his reign at one of its most critical times.

Since Lu'lu''s policy is unknown, his career cannot be described in terms of its evolution. The following account therefore necessarily centers on his relations with his three most prominent neighbors, the Ayyubids, the Caliph, and the Mongols, for whom the historical record is more complete.

Ayyubid Relations and Expansion into the Jazīra

For some time after the Caliph's recognition of Lu'lu' as sultan, Mosul remained loyal to the Ayyubid rulers al-Kāmil and al-Ashraf. Lu'lu' retained the title Atabeg, hitherto borne (in Mosul) only by the Zangids, and substituted his name for that of the Zangid Atabeg on the city's coinage. There are only a few reports concerning Lu'lu's first years as sultan, for the histories focus on the continuing Mongol raids, and the military activities of the Ayyubids as they attempted to reestablish their authority in the Jazīra and Armenia. The Mongols had defeated the Khwārazm Shāh Jalāl al-Dīn in 628/1231 and scattered his army throughout the region. Jalāl al-Dīn was killed in the course of his flight to safety, and henceforth his leaderless troops "moved from pasture to pasture, eating and drinking,"[1] causing many problems for the established rulers of the Jazīra. When al-Kāmil and al-Ashraf died within a few months of each other in 635/1237–38, the stage was set for a long period of political instability as the Khwārazmians, Lu'lu', and various Ayyubid and Artuqid rulers vied for power and fought each other for possession of the Jazīra.

Before al-Kāmil's death, his son al-Ṣāliḥ Ayyūb had attracted the allegiance of the Khwārazmian mercenaries and with their aid had displaced al-Ashraf's successors from the Jazīra. The Khwārazmians raided into Mosul's territory, forcing Lu'lu' to pay tribute to al-Ṣāliḥ in an effort to achieve security on his border, but the Khwārazmians persisted in their harassment. After al-Kāmil's death, the Ayyubid confederation was left without a paramount leader. The Khwārazmians abandoned

1. Al-Makīn Ibn al-ʿAmīd, 149.

al-Ṣāliḥ and entered the service of the Artuqid ruler of Mārdīn. They then occupied most of the Jazīra and engaged in extensive looting. Al-Ṣāliḥ sought refuge in Sinjār, where Lu'lu' besieged him in Dhu'l-Qa'da 635/June–July 1237 after capturing Naṣībīn. Of his career to date, this act was the most aggressive—his first bid for territorial expansion at Ayyubid expense.[2] Al-Ṣāliḥ was beset not only by the Khwārazmians, but by the rulers of Rūm, Aleppo, Mārdīn, and Mayyāfāriqīn, who wished to divide the Jazīra among themselves. Whether a part of this alliance or not, Lu'lu' obviously wished to profit from al-Ṣāliḥ's weakness to obtain a share of the spoils. Al-Ṣāliḥ sued for peace, but Lu'lu' refused, saying that he wished "to take him in a cage to Baghdad," a statement which implies that Lu'lu' regarded al-Ṣāliḥ's rule as unlawful.[3]

Al-Ṣāliḥ sent the qadi of Sinjār in disguise through Lu'lu''s lines to negotiate with the Khwārazmians and regain their support. On his behalf, the qadi granted the *iqṭā'* of Ḥarrān, al-Ruhā, and much of the Jazīra to the Khwārazmians, and promised them Naṣībīn as well when they recaptured it from Lu'lu'. The Khwārazmians accepted the offer and quickly rode to Sinjār. Mosul's army was surprised in its camp and badly defeated; Lu'lu' himself was barely able to escape to Mosul. His camp and treasury, including a great number of luxury items, were captured. The Khwārazmians occupied Naṣībīn without difficulty. With Khwārazmian support, al-Ṣāliḥ secured his position

2. Lu'lu' acknowledged no Ayyubid overlord for five years after the deaths of al-Kāmil and al-Ashraf. His attempt to occupy Sinjār may be seen as an effort to exploit Ayyubid weakness.

3. Perhaps because he had forcibly ejected al-Ashraf's successors from the city. See Sibṭ, 466; al-Birzālī, f. 416a.

in the Jazīra and he and Lu'lu' agreed to peace on terms of mutual respect for each other's territory.[4]

Al-Ṣāliḥ's star continued to rise. The position of the Ayyubid ruler of Damascus, al-Jawād Yūnus, had grown increasingly untenable during the course of 635. Hard pressed by his rival al-ʿĀdil, al-Kāmil's son and successor in Egypt, to relinquish his authority, al-Jawād decided instead to give the city to al-Ṣāliḥ in exchange for Sinjār, al-Raqqa, and ʿĀna. Al-Ṣāliḥ accepted the offer, and arrived in Damascus on Friday, 29 Jumādā I 636/7 January 1239. Badr al-Dīn Lu'lu' sent with him forty uniformed mamluks with horses, equipment, and money to help ensure his success. Lu'lu' was perhaps delighted to see the resourceful Ayyubid established at a greater distance from Mosul and replaced by a far less competent individual. Lu'lu''s contribution of a force of mamluks to support al-Ṣāliḥ, and the friendly relationship existing between the two rulers thereafter,[5] suggests the extent to which the success of both rulers was related to the growing power of mamluks.

Al-Jawād experienced some difficulty establishing himself in Sinjār. Since he had taken the treasury of Damascus with him when he left, al-Ṣāliḥ asked the

4. Sibṭ, 465–66; Ibn al-ʿAdīm, 3:241–43; al-Makīn Ibn al-ʿAmīd, 149; Ibn Khallikān, 5:92; Ibn Shaddād, *Aʿlāq* ff. 17b, 35a–b; Ibn Wāṣil, 5:147, 153, 178–79, 186–88; Qirṭāy, f. 13b; al-Yūnīnī, 2:332; al-Birzālī, f. 416a; al-Dhahabī, *Taʾrīkh al-Islām*, Bodl. MS Laud 305, f. 12b.

5. A token of this friendship was Lu'lu''s protection of al-Ṣāliḥ's mamluk Fāris al-Dīn Aqṭāy al-Mustaʿrab (d. 673) during al-Ṣāliḥ's brief captivity in al-Karak in 637 (Ibn Shaddād, *Ẓāhir*, 113). Lu'lu' also aided al-Ṣāliḥ's son Tūrānshāh with mamluks and equipment in 643 (Sibṭ, 500) and militarily in 644 (al-Dhahabī, *Taʾrīkh al-Islām*, Bodl. MS Laud 305, f. 161a). As a mamluk, Lu'lu' had much to gain by supporting the career of the Ayyubid ruler most dependent on mamluk support for his success.

Khwārazmians to arrest him as he entered the Jazīra, but al-Jawād evaded capture and went to ʿĀna. Meanwhile, Lu'lu' besieged Sinjār, but was driven off by Khwārazmian mercenaries in the pay of al-Jawād.[6] Al-Jawād's troubles did not end with his arrival in Sinjār. He was very unpopular with his subjects, and, perhaps in an effort to consolidate his position, he tried to arrange a marriage with a daughter of Lu'lu'. Lu'lu' used the proposal as an opportunity to gain entrance into the city and sieze control of it.[7] Lu'lu' occupied the city in Rabīʿ I 637/October 1239 and named his son al-Malik al-Muẓaffar ʿAlā' al-Dīn ʿAlī its governor. Al-Jawād fled to Baghdad, and soon sold ʿĀna, his only remaining territory, to the Caliph in an effort to remain solvent.

The situation in the Jazīra remained extremely unstable. Al-Jawād now joined with the Khwārazmians and other dispossessed Ayyubid princes in an apparent effort to seize control of the Jazīra. They defeated a small force from Aleppo near al-Bīra in Ṣafar or Rabīʿ I 638/September 1240, capturing or killing some of the leading members of the Aleppo branch of the Ayyubid family. Shortly thereafter, they captured Manbaj, thus acquiring control of an important fort that guarded the approach to the Jazīra from Aleppo. The rulers of Aleppo quickly assembled additional forces from Ḥimṣ and Damascus and drove the Khwārazmians from the west bank of the

6. Ibn al-ʿAdīm, 3:245; Ibn Shaddād, *Aʿlāq*, f. 36a; Ibn Wāṣil, 5:200–4; *Ḥawādith*, 114; Qirṭāy, f. 16b.

7. Al-Makīn Ibn al-ʿAmīd, 152. The accounts of this incident differ widely. The feature common to most is that Lu'lu''s men gained entrance to the city through some ruse while al-Jawād was absent, and seized it with the support of part of its population. Cf. Sibṭ, 483; Ibn al-ʿAdīm, 3:245; Ibn Shaddād, *Aʿlāq*, ff. 36a–b; Ibn Wāṣil, 5:253; *Ḥawādith*, 121–22; al-Ghassānī, 490–91.

Euphrates. Then in Ramaḍān 638/April 1241 they routed the Khwārazmians near al-Ruhā. The Khwārazmians escaped to 'Āna, now a domain of the Caliph. Lu'lu' moved swiftly to occupy Naṣībīn and Dārā in their wake. The Khwārazmians had imprisoned the captured Ayyubids at Dārā, and Lu'lu' won control of the town through their mediation. His right to possess it was later confirmed by the ruler of Aleppo, the eleven-year-old al-Nāṣir Yūsuf. The rest of the Jazīra was divided among the Ayyubid rulers of Ḥimṣ and Aleppo, and the Rūm Saljuq Kaykhusraw.[8]

The Khwārazmians returned to the Jazīra the following year, having allied with the Ayyubid ruler of Mayyāfāriqīn, Shihāb al-Dīn Ghāzī. They took control of Naṣībīn from Lu'lu' and went on to invade the territory of Amid, held by the Saljuqs. In Ṣafar 639/August–September 1241 the army of Aleppo entered the Jazīra, drove the Khwārazmians and Ghāzī away from Amid, and pursued them into the area around Mayyāfāriqīn. There an allied force composed of units from Rūm, Aleppo, Mosul, Mārdīn, Malatya, and the Jazīra defeated the Khwārazmians. Hostilities ceased for a time while a truce was negotiated, but the parties could not agree on terms, so the Khwārazmians again returned to looting in the territories

8. Ibn al-'Adīm, 3:259–60; Ibn Bībī, 216; Ibn Shaddād, *A'lāq*, ff. 15a, 17b, 25a, 26a, 70b; Ibn Wāṣil, 5:281–96; *Ḥawādith*, 143. After the Khwārazmian defeat, Kaykhusraw joined the victors and annexed Amid, a city belonging to a son of al-Ṣāliḥ Ayyūb. Kaykhusraw's name appears on some of Mosul's coins for 638 and 640, and all of those for 639, which suggests that Lu'lu' preferred to extend his domains in the Jazīra under the aegis of the Saljuqs rather than any of the quarrelling Ayyubids. (Coins of Mosul bearing Kaykhusraw's name are published under the date 637 as well, but I believe these should be re-examined to confirm that the word read as "seven" is not really "nine.") On the coins, see Artuq, 413; Edhem, 106–7; Hennequin, 252–54; al-Ḥusaynī, 58–59; Lane-Poole, 9:305.

of Mosul in Jumādā I 639/November–December 1241, capturing Naṣībīn and Ra's al-ʿAyn. Lu'lu' asked for and received some help from the Caliph to drive them off, but each time they returned.

The army of Aleppo again entered the Jazīra and drove the Khwārazmians from the territories they had occupied. They recaptured Naṣībīn and gave half its territory to Lu'lu' and retained the other half for themselves. The Khwāraziams first withdrew to Mayyāfāriqīn, but then returned to the Jazīra with their ally Ghāzī. They were pursued and defeated by the army of Aleppo near Majdal in Ṣafar 640/August 1242.

This battle was a resounding defeat for the Khwārazmians, and seems to have effectively demonstrated Ayyubid domination of the Jazīra. Although the Khwārazmians retained some power, and soon returned to looting at Ra's al-ʿAyn and in the Khābūr, they were never again a major threat to the security of the Jazīra. Al-Nāṣir apparently recognized their control of the region by assigning them his share of the *iqṭāʿ* of Naṣībīn.[9] Lu'lu' too accepted Ayyubid authority, and replaced the name of the Rūm Saljuq ruler with that of the al-Nāṣir on Mosul's coins of the year 640.[10] This settlement of the long struggle for control of the Jazīra was evidently not to Khwārazmians' liking, for they suddenly abandoned the region in 642/1244, probably intending to join al-Ṣāliḥ Ayyūb in Egypt, or at least avoid the Mongols, who had appeared again in strength in Anatolia.[11]

9. Sibṭ, 488; Ibn al-ʿAdīm, 3:260–64; Ibn Bībī, 220; Ibn Shaddād, *Aʿlāq*, ff. 25a, 70b–71a; Ibn Wāṣil, 5:304–5, 309–11; al-Dhahabī, *Ta'rīkh al-Islām*, Bodl. MS Laud 305, ff. 16b–17a; al-Ghassānī, 501; *Ḥawādith*, 151.

10. Hennequin, 254; al-Ḥusaynī, 59.

11. Ibn Shaddād, *Aʿlaq*, f. 25a; Ibn Wāṣil, 5:323–25; Cahen, *Pre-Ottoman Turkey*, 138.

From Lu'lu''s point of view, their departure simply substituted one difficulty for another. Al-Nāṣir redistributed the Khwārazmian's *iqṭā'*, forcing Lu'lu' to share Naṣībīn with al-Malik al-Sa'īd, the Artuqid ruler of Mārdīn, and al-Mu'aẓẓam Tūrānshāh of Ḥiṣn Kayfā. Lu'lu' and al-Sa'īd were to quarrel over Naṣībīn and neighboring Dārā for several years to come. Their shared rule was interrupted in 642/1244 by Ghāzī of Mayyāfāriqīn, who occupied Naṣībīn temporarily while his own city was occupied by the Mongols. After he returned to Mayyāfāriqīn in 643, al-Sa'īd occupied Naṣībīn and held it alone until 645, when negotiations undertaken by the Caliph restored the former state of shared possession with Lu'lu'. Perhaps because of his dissatisfaction with the Ayyubid position concerning Naṣībīn, Lu'lu' dropped al-Nāṣir's name from Mosul's coinage in 641 and reinstated that of the Rūm Saljuq Kaykhusraw until the latter's death in 644. Thereafter Lu'lu' acknowledged no overlord for several years.[12] Perhaps in an effort to regain Lu'lu''s allegiance, al-Nāṣir ceded to Mosul the Khābūr region, including the important town of Qarqīsiyā, following the death of its ruler, al-Manṣūr of Ḥimṣ, in 644/1246.[13] But although this addition nearly doubled the amount of territory under Lu'lu''s control, he did not acknowledge al-Nāṣir's supremacy.

When a civil war erupted between al-Nāṣir of Aleppo and al-Ṣāliḥ Ayyūb of Egypt in 646/1248, al-Sa'īd and Lu'lu' took opposite sides and fought each other over the control of Naṣībīn. Lu'lu' looted around Dunaysir and

12. Artuq, 413; Edhem, 108; Hennequin, 254–56; Lane-Poole, 9:305.

13. Ibn Shaddād, *A'lāq*, ff. 25a–27b; al-Dhahabī (quoting the lost history of Sa'd al-Dīn Juwaynī), *Ta'rīkh al-Islām*, Bodl. MS Laud 305, ff. 158a–b (cf. Cahen, "Une source pour l'histoire des croisades," 328).

defeated al-Sa'īd's army near Ra's al-'Ayn. He occupied all of Naṣībīn and showed his determination to remain in possession by strengthening the fortifications of its citadel and establishing a treasury there. Al-Sa'īd called upon al-Nāṣir, and with his help defeated Lu'lu' near Naṣībīn on 7 Rabī' II 646/30 July 1248. Lu'lu''s camp and treasury were captured; within three months he had lost control not only of Naṣībīn, but of Dārā and the Khābūr region as well. Lu'lu' appealed to the Caliph to mediate, and soon an agreement acceptable to all was achieved. Lu'lu' agreed to cede Dārā and part of the Khābūr to al-Sa'īd in exchange for control of all of Naṣībīn. He was required to pay an annual tribute to al-Nāṣir and proclaim his subordination to the Ayyubid ruler in Mosul's *khuṭba* and on its coins.[14]

But neither al-Nāṣir's victory nor the subsequent death of al-Ṣāliḥ Ayyūb in Sha'bān 647/November 1249 made Lu'lu' a more willing subordinate. The death of al-Nāṣir's rival in Egypt only increased his problems. Al-Ṣāliḥ's son Tūrānshāh ruled only a short time before he was assassinated by his mamluks on 28 Muḥarram 648/2 May 1250.[15] Thereafter, Egypt's affairs were dominated by a group of mamluks led by a Bahriya officer named 'Izz al-Dīn Aybak. Al-Nāṣir began preparations to invade Egypt to reestablish Ayyubid control, with support from Mosul under the command of Lu'lu''s son al-Muẓaffar 'Alī. When the Egyptians defeated al-Nāṣir in Dhu'l-Qa'da 648/February 1251, Lu'lu' remained loyal and ordered

14. Some of Mosul's coins for 648 bear the name of al-Nāṣir. See Hennequin, 258–59.

15. One of the mamluks, Fāris al-Dīn Aqṭāyā, joined the conspiracy when he learned that Tūrānshāh was planning to send him to Mosul, ostensibly as an envoy, but actually to have Lu'lu' arrest him.

al-Muẓaffar to remain in al-Nāṣir's service.[16] Al-Nāṣir had no success in mustering his forces to meet the mamluk emergency. The remaining years of his rule were spent in a fruitless effort to retain control of his own territories against a series of rebellions.

While al-Nāṣir was preoccupied with his troubles, Lu'lu' now chose to move against the last remaining Zangid principality, Jazīrat b. ʿUmar. Its ruler al-Malik al-Muʿaẓẓam Maḥmūd had died at the end of 648/1251 after a reign of more than forty years.[17] He had enjoyed good relations with the Ayyubids, and as additional security had married his son and successor al-Masʿūd Shāhānshāh to a daughter of Lu'lu'. When al-Masʿūd came to the throne, relations with Mosul grew strained. Al-Masʿūd sent an envoy to al-Nāṣir complaining about hostility from Mosul, and al-Nāṣir dispatched his envoy Ibn Shaddād to negotiate a resolution of the difficulties. Ibn Shaddād gives a detailed and fascinating account of his reception in Mosul in 649/1251.[18] When he received Ibn Shaddād, Lu'lu' made various allegations about al-Masʿūd's conduct. He complained in particular that the Zangid had taught his wife—Lu'lu''s daughter—obscene language, which he wanted the envoy to hear for himself. Ibn Shaddād refused, but Lu'lu' pressed him to convey to al-Nāṣir an offer of fifty thousand dinars for permission to take control of Jazīrat b. ʿUmar. (From other sources we learn that

16. Ibn Shaddād, *Aʿlāq*, f. 41a (see the Appendix); Ibn Taghribirdī, 7:10.

17. Ibn Shaddād, *Aʿlāq*, f. 41a (cf. Amedroz, 802; Cahen, "Djazira," 121); al-Ṣafadī, *Al-Wāfī bi'l-wafayāt*, vol. 3, ed. Sven Dedering, Bibliotheca Islamica, vol. 6c (Wiesbaden: Franz Steiner Verlag, 1953), 140.

18. *Aʿlāq*, ff. 41a–43a; cf. Amedroz, 803–5. A translation is presented in the Appendix.

Lu'lu' also accused al-Masʿūd of interfering with Mosul's claims concerning Naṣībīn.[19]) Lu'lu' may have threatened to renounce his allegiance to al-Nāṣir, for Ibn Shaddād reports that he scolded Lu'lu' for refusing the robe and standard of al-Nāṣir.

Lu'lu' eventually grew dissatisfied with the progress of his negotiations with Ibn Shaddād and dismissed the envoy, who continued on with his mission by going to Jazīrat b. ʿUmar to call on al-Masʿūd. As soon as Ibn Shaddād was out of Mosul, Lu'lu' opened negotiations with Majd al-Dīn Ibn al-ʿAdīm, who was already in Mosul (apparently to represent al-Nāṣir at the funeral of Lu'lu''s eldest son Amīn al-Dīn[20]). Ibn al-ʿAdīm wrote on Lu'lu''s behalf to his father Kamāl al-Dīn in Syria, and the latter arranged for Lu'lu''s son al-Muẓaffar to meet with an envoy of the Caliph and al-Nāṣir to discuss terms for the transfer of Jazīrat b. ʿUmar to Lu'lu'. Meanwhile, Ibn Shaddād was received in Jazīra by al-Masʿūd, who was so desperate that he wanted the envoy to hold his city for him while he went in person to Syria to talk to al-Nāṣir. Ibn Shaddād refused, and soon went on to Mārdīn to fulfill another part of his mission. Al-Nāṣir agreed to allow Lu'lu' to take control of Jazīra, on condition that he wait until the mamluk revolt in Egypt had been quelled, but Lu'lu' disregarded the condition and captured Jazīra after a three week siege on Friday, 11 Rajab

19. Ibn al-ʿIbrī, 261; Bar Hebraeus, 1:420–21; al-Dhahabī, *Ta'rīkh al-Islām*, Bodl. MS 305, f. 166b. Bar Hebraeus's account is dated to 647, but the two dates he records fit better in the year 649.

20. Ibn Shaddād, *A'lāq*, f. 41b. Ibn Wāṣil (Bibl. Nat. MS 1703, f. 108a) reports that Ibn al-ʿAdīm was in Mosul to mediate between the rulers of Mosul and Mārdīn over the control of Naṣībīn. He dates Ibn al-ʿAdīm's mission of consolation to 652 (Bibl. Nat. MS 1703, f. 112b). The dispute over Naṣībīn, however, had been settled in 647.

649/29 September 1251. Lu'lu' arrested al-Mas'ūd and sent him in a boat toward Mosul, but arranged to have him drowned on the way. He bestowed the government of the town on his son al-Mujāhid Sayf al-Dīn Isḥāq, and established a treasury and mint there.[21]

Lu'lu''s realm was now at its greatest extent, and included Kurdistan, Sinjār, Jazīrat b. 'Umar, Naṣībīn, and the Khābūr district as far as Qarqīsiyā.[22] The dispute with al-Sa'īd over Naṣībīn erupted once more in 651/1253 when al-Sa'īd captured the town, but Lu'lu' recovered it again in the following year as the consequence of negotiations undertaken by al-Nāṣir's envoy Kamāl al-Dīn Ibn al-'Adīm.[23] Lu'lu' would continue to hold the town for the rest of his reign. Although Lu'lu' acknowledged the supremacy of al-Nāṣir on nearly all his coins for the years 649 to 656, the histories record few details of his relations with the Ayyubids. There is some evidence that, as the Ayyubid rulers became increasingly preoccupied with their declining fortunes in Syria, Lu'lu' sought to improve his relations with the mamluks.

21. Artuk, 412; Edhem, 112; Hennequin, 247–48; al-Ḥusaynī, 122; Lane-Poole, 3:206. Edhem, Artuk, and al-Ḥusaynī have dated some of their specimens to 647. I believe these coins should be reexamined in view of the well known tendency to confuse the Arabic words "seven" and "nine." It seems reasonably certain that al-Mu'aẓẓam did not die until 648, and all accounts agree that Lu'lu' took over the city from the Zangid's successor, Shāhānshāh.

22. Ibn Shaddād, *A'lāq*, f. 27b; al-Yūnīnī, 2:310. Remains of the bridge built over the Khābūr River at 'Arabān, near Qarqīsiyā, during Lu'lu''s reign survive, see *RCEA* 12:36–37 (no. 4453).

23. Ibn Shaddād, *A'lāq*, f. 25b; cf. Cahen, "Djazira," 121. Another possible reference to this incident is in Rashīd al-Dīn (*Successors*, 233), but this could equally well be a misdating of the 647 battle. See also Ibn Wāṣil, Bibl. Nat. MS 1703, f. 112b.

In 655/1257 he entered negotiations with the mamluk ʿIzz al-Dīn Aybak of Egypt regarding the latter's marriage to a daughter of Lu'lu'. Nothing came of the proposal, for it engendered such alarm among the Ayyubid faction in Egypt that Aybak was soon assassinated. Nevertheless, the negotiations serve to indicate Lu'lu''s waning support of al-Nāṣir and his renewed devotion to the cause of mamluks. During the same period of time, the Mongols were preparing to resume their conquests in western Asia, thereby forcing Lu'lu' to improve his relations with them at the expense of his loyalty to al-Nāṣir.

Lu'lu''s relations with the Ayyubids after the deaths of al-Ashraf and al-Kāmil were clearly based on his desire to extend his authority over the Jazīra at their expense, but with no native historian to record his perspective, his motivation and justification can only be dimly perceived. The historians on whom one must rely represented Mosul simply as a military force of some strength, and Lu'lu' as a figure to be swayed sometimes by force and sometimes by diplomacy. The Ayyubids could not recover Sinjār from Lu'lu' because they required his cooperation to cope with the much greater threat posed by the Khwārazmians. After Aleppo defeated the Khwārazmians in 640, Lu'lu' was forced briefly to acknowledge Ayyubid supremacy, but his rivalry with the ruler of Mārdīn over Naṣībīn rendered continued subordination intolerable. The settlement of the Naṣībīn problem in 646 entailed renewed subordination to the Ayyubids, but by that time their confederation was crumbling and his subordination was of only nominal significance. Lu'lu' exploited Ayyubid weakness further in 649, when, under the guise of subordination, he occupied Jazīrat b. ʿUmar. Thereafter the histories shift their attention from Mosul to the dramatic events in Syria, Egypt, and Iran.

Relations with Baghdad

Mosul's relations with Baghdad were peaceful throughout this era. For the most part, the history of the contacts between the two cities is one of social and diplomatic exchanges, through which Lu'lu' probably sought to win the Caliph's support in his conflicts and generally maintain his prestige throughout the region. As the legitimizer of governmental authority, the name of the Caliph was proclaimed on coinage and in the *khuṭba* of Mosul, the Ayyubid states, and nearly all other Muslim governments. More practically, the Caliph negotiated truces and mediated disputes between rulers, for which his envoys frequently met with Lu'lu', particularly in connection with the dispute over Naṣībīn. Finally, Mosul and Baghdad shared a common border and both faced Iran, from which the Mongols occasionally launched raids into their territories. Military cooperation was sometimes necessary, and both Lu'lu' and the Caliph sent armies on joint expeditions to ward off Mongol attacks.

Diplomatic marriages were an important part of the maintenance of good relations. As mentioned previously, a daughter of Lu'lu' married the Caliph's amir al-Duwaydār al-Kabīr in 625/1227–28. In 632/1234 another of Lu'lu''s daughters was betrothed to Mujāhid al-Dīn Aybak al-Khāṣṣ al-Mustanṣirī, known as al-Duwaydār al-Ṣaghīr (the son of al-Duwaydār al-Kabīr).[24] The marriage took place in Jumādā II 634/February 1237. The first son of this marriage, Ghāzī, grew up to assume a position among Baghdad's elite in the years before the Mongol conquest.[25] These marriages were celebrated at great expense

24. *Ḥawādith*, 72–73, 92; al-Ghassānī, 465–66, 475–76, 633; al-Dhahabī, *Ta'rīkh al-Islām*, Bodl. MS Laud 305, f. 12; MS Laud 279, f. 82b.

25. Al-Ghassānī, 549–50, 544.

and with elaborate ceremony, and provided an occasion for social contact between Lu'lu''s sons and representatives and members of the Caliph's court. In Rabīʿ I 633/December 1235 Lu'lu''s son al-Ṣāliḥ Ismāʿīl went to Baghdad to visit his sister who was married to al-Duwaydār al-Kabīr.[26]

Another form of social contact involved the ceremonies of the *futuwwa* order. The exact significance of these events is not explained in our sources, but it is clear that the leaders of Mosul and Baghdad shared to some extent a common ethical perspective. In 634/1236 Lu'lu''s son al-Ṣāliḥ Ismāʿīl, while engaging in a form of ritual hunting (*ramy al-bunduq*) permitted only to *futuwwa* initiates, killed a bird belonging to the Baghdad amir Sharaf al-Dīn al-Sharrābī. His servants went to Baghdad and presented the bird to its owner, for which they were richly rewarded. This incident followed upon a visit to Baghdad earlier in the year by al-Ṣāliḥ himself, with a considerable entourage.[27] Al-Ṣāliḥ's visits may have also been related to a state visit to Baghdad by the Zangid Nūr al-Dīn Arslān Shāh III, who had succeeded to the throne of Shahrazūr after his father ʿImād al-Dīn Zankī's death in 633/1236. The amir al-Sharrabī had at that time presented him with the ceremonial garments of the *futuwwa* order, and may have thereby caused Lu'lu' some anxiety about the possibility of a renewal of Zangid claims to the rule of Mosul.[28] In 638/1240–41 an indi-

26. Bar Hebraeus, 1:402; *Ḥawādith*, 79–81; al-Ghassānī, 471.

27. *Ḥawādith*, 95–96; al-Dhahabī, *Ta'rīkh al-Islām*, Bodl. MS Laud 305, f. 12a; al-Ghassānī, 474.

28. It was probably on the occasion of this visit to Mosul (5–15 Ṣafar 634/8–18 October 1236) that Arslān Shāh commissioned the historian Ibn al-Sāʿī to write the *Muʿallim al-Atābakiya*, a work celebrating the glorious history of the Zangid dynasty. See Patton, "Ibn

vidual identified as the amir Ibrāhīm b. Badr al-Dīn Lu'lu' (perhaps Lu'lu''s son Amīn al-Dīn) killed a bird while hunting. It was sent to Baghdad, where its deliverers received lavish honors.[29] Since membership in the *futuwwa* was an important symbol of loyalty to the Caliph, these occasions illustrate the importance which the ruler of Mosul attached to his ties with Baghdad.

Funerals were also occasions for ceremonial visits between Mosul and Baghdad. When the daughter of Lu'lu' who had married al-Duwaydār al-Kabīr died in childbirth in Rabī' II 635/November–December 1237, her funeral at the Shrine of Mūsā b. Ja'far al-Kāẓim was attended by the most important notables of Baghdad.[30] The Caliph sent his envoy 'Abd al-Raḥman Ibn al-Jawzī to Mosul to attend ceremonies of mourning held there. When the Caliph al-Mustanṣir died in Jumādā II 640/5 November 1242, Lu'lu' sent his son al-Ṣāliḥ Ismā'īl to Baghdad to attend the ceremony of mourning and to present the Caliph al-Musta'ṣim with a thousand dinars for funeral expenses.[31]

The 630's appear to have been the heyday of Mosul's relations with Baghdad. Lu'lu' does not seem to have enjoyed the same close relationship with the court of al-Musta'ṣim as he did with that of al-Mustanṣir. The closeness of the 630's was most likely related to

---

al-Sā'ī's Account," 151–53. Arslān Shāh visited Baghdad two more times in 635/1237 and once in 640/1242. He died on 14 Sha'bān 642/15 January 1245. Shahrazūr was given to an amir of the Caliph, Falak al-Dīn Muḥammad b. Sunqur al-Ṭawīl, from whom the Mongols captured the city four months later. See Ibn al-Sā'ī, *Mu'allim*, f. 82b; al-Dhahabī, *Ta'rīkh al-Islām*, Bodl. MS Laud 305, ff. 158b, 174b; *Ḥawādith*, 88–89, 110–11, 165; al-Ṣafadī, 8:343; al-Ghassānī, 481, 532–33.

29. *Ḥawādith*, 143.

30. *Ḥawādith*, 101, 264–65.

31. *Ḥawādith*, 165; al-Ghassānī, 512.

Lu'lu''s desire to sustain his independence from the Ayyubids and expand his domains in the Jazīra. But he may also have been engaged in a "public relations" war with the Zangids of Shahrazūr, whose rule over Mosul Lu'lu' had boldly usurped twenty years before. The Zangids could not be combatted directly since they had become direct clients of the Caliph after the death of Kūkburī in 630. Finally, good relations were further stimulated by the pressure of the occasional Mongol raids into Iraq, especially in the mid 630's.

The Rise of Mongol Influence

Summary accounts of the Mongol conquest of Iraq often leave the impression that it was a single swift and devastating invasion. Actually the invasion took place only after a forty year period in which raids, small invasions, diplomatic pressure, and complete inactivity alternated with little apparent pattern. Badr al-Dīn Lu'lu' is perhaps the only ruler whose reign spanned almost the entire period of Mongol encroachment, from their first raid into Iraq in 618/1221 until the occupation of Iraq was completed with the capture of Mosul in 660/1262. His response to the growing Mongol threat is interesting to observe. It is apparent that in the 630's he was preoccupied with territorial expansion in the Jazīra and did not consider the Mongols to be more than an occasional nuisance. His attitude appears to have been justified by the uncoordinated and sporadic nature of Mongol activities in the Near East prior to the death of the Khan Ögedei in 639/1241. Thereafter the Mongols showed renewed interest in the conquest of western Asia, forcing Lu'lu' and other rulers to take Mongol activity more seriously.

Mosul's early contacts with the Mongols have been mentioned above. The Mongol generals Jebe and Sübedei raided into Iraq in 618/1221 during the course of their invasion of Adharbayjān. Mosul's forces joined with those of Irbil and Baghdad in an expedition to keep the Mongol party under surveillance, but there was apparently no fighting and the Mongols soon returned to Adharbayjān. The second phase of Mongol activity began in 628/1230, when Adharbayjān was permanently reoccupied under the *noyan* (commander) Chormaghun. The Mongols defeated the Khwārazmian army near Amid and pursued its remnants through the Jazīra.[32] The Khwārazmian leader Jalāl al-Dīn was killed near Mayyāfāriqīn in the course of his flight to safety. The Mongols also entered Iraq directly from Adharbayjān and raided in the vicinity of Irbil in 628 and 629 (1231–32).[33] These raids caused much panic in Mosul, leading some people to leave the city for Syria. A regrettably brief reference in the history of Ibn Naẓīf al-Ḥamawī notes that in 631 the Caliph gave his permission for Mongol agents to establish a permanent residence in Mosul.[34] Ibn Bāṭīsh reports that the Mongols came to Mosul in 632/1234–35 and also that Lu'lu', perhaps not coincidentally, strengthened Mosul's fortifications in this year.[35]

Mongol activity grew ever more ominous. In Rabī' I 633/November–December 1235 the Mongols skirmished with the garrison of Irbil, raided in the Nineveh district of Mosul, and then continued west through the Jazīra. They raided around Sinjār, killing its wazīr Mu'īn al-Dīn Ibn Kamāl al-Dīn Ibn Muhājir at the gates of the city, and

32. *Kāmil*, 12:497–501; Ibn Naẓīf, ff. 210a–b; Bar Hebraeus, 1:396–97.

33. *Kāmil*, 12:501–3; Bar Hebraeus, 1:396–97; *Ḥawādith*, 27–30; al-Dhahabī, *Ta'rīkh al-Islām*, Bodl. MS Laud 305, ff. 9a–b.

34. F. 226b.

35. Ed. al-Māni', 2:124.

then, before returning to Adharbayjān, massacred a caravan of merchants bound for Syria.[36] In Shawwāl 634/June 1237 the Mongols returned again to Iraq and besieged Irbil—their first attempt to capture a major Iraqi city. They forced Lu'lu' to contribute supplies to support their efforts. The Caliph sent an army under al-Duwaydār al-Ṣaghīr, Lu'lu''s son-in-law, to relieve the city, but before it arrived the city was captured and looted. After the capture of the town, the citadel held out for forty days, until the Mongols abandoned their siege in Dhu'l-Ḥijja 634/July–August 1237.[37] Another raid into Iraq was launched at the end of the same summer (635/1237).[38]

The Mongols then became inactive in the region for some time, perhaps because of the need to concentrate their forces in Russia for a major series of conquests underway there. This proved to be a blessing for Mosul since these were the years in which Lu'lu', the Ayyubids, and the Khwārazmians fought over the control of the Jazīra. Mosul's reprieve ended when the *noyan* Baiju replaced Chormaghun (incapacitated through illness) as military commander of western Iran in 639/1242.[39] Under his command, the Mongols launched a major invasion into the Saljuq territories of Erzerum and Erzinjān in Anatolia.[40] On 6 Muḥarram 641/26 June 1243 they defeated

36. Sibṭ, 460; Ibn al-'Ibrī, 250; Bar Hebraeus, 1:402; *Ḥawādith*, 84–85; al-Dhahabī, *Ta'rīkh al-Islām*, Bodl. MS Laud 305, ff. 11b–12a; al-Ghassānī, 470.

37. Sibṭ, 462; Ibn Khallikān, 4:149; Ibn al-'Ibrī, 250; Bar Hebraeus, 1:402; *Ḥawādith*, 98–99; al-Dhahabī, *Ta'rīkh al-Islām*, Bodl. MS Laud 305, f. 12b; al-Ṣafadī, 10:66–67; al-Ghassānī, 478.

38. Bar Hebraeus, 1:404; *Ḥawādith*, 109–10; al-Ghassānī, 479.

39. See Jackson, "Dissolution of the Mongol Empire," 216–17.

40. Baiju was a client of Batu, the leader of the Jochid house of the Mongol ruling family, to whom Chingiz Khan had allotted the rule of

the Saljuqs at Köse Dagh and broke their power forever. Mongol military pressure was felt in the Jazīra the next year, when they raided as far south as Sinjār.[41] Then at the end of 642/1245 they captured Shahrazūr,[42] and the following summer (643/1245) they raided in the Caliph's domains north of Baghdad.[43]

This resurgence of military activity had its effect on the rulers of Mosul and Syria. The historian Ibn Wāṣil learned of the Saljuq's defeat at Köse Dagh from Lu'lu' while in Mosul en route to Syria after a diplomatic mission in Baghdad. He makes the surprising statement that Lu'lu' was then obedient to the Mongols, with whom he corresponded and exchanged presents.[44] This can not have been obedience in the formal sense, because Mosul's coins proclaim only the Caliph as overlord, but it is safe to assume that Lu'lu' had been impressed by the Mongols' capture of Irbil and wished to avoid a similar fate for Mosul. The Mongols clearly considered Mosul to be under their control, for Juvaynī specifically mentions Mosul among the territories entrusted to the governor Arghun by the Regent Törägänä in 641/1243–44.[45] The terms of

---

Western Asia (including Iran) and Europe. Mongol expedition commanders were customarily accompanied by representatives of each of the four Mongol ruling families, and Baiju had the status of second-in-command to Chormaghun because western Asia was part of Batu's territory. During the interval between Ögedei's death in 639/1241 and the election of a new Khan, Batu apparently pressed Baiju to extend Mongol conquests in his name into Anatolia, Syria, and the Jazīra. See Jackson, "Dissolution of the Mongol Empire," 215–19; Allsen, 59; Ibn al-ʿAdīm, 3:263; Ibn Shaddād, *Aʿlāq*, f. 25a; Ibn Wāṣil, 5:310.

41. Al-Dhahabī, *Ta'rīkh al-Islām*, Bodl. MS Laud 305, f. 158b.

42. Al-Dhahabī, *Ta'rīkh al-Islām*, Bodl. MS Laud 305, f. 158b; al-Ghassānī, 533.

43. *Ḥawādith*, 199–200.

44. Ibn Wāṣil, 5:324–25.

45. 2:507.

Mosul's obedience are not apparent, but whatever control the Mongols exerted did not prevent Lu'lu' from further improvement of Mosul's fortifications.[46]

Revenue was probably among their principal concerns, but although Lu'lu' had probably been paying tribute for some time, there is no reference to it in the histories. The earliest reference is dated to 642/1244–45, when Lu'lu' forwarded to Damascus a Mongol demand that its citizens pay an annual assessment (*qaṭī'a*), at the rates of ten dirhems for the rich, five for the middle-class, and one for the poor.[47] The order was read publicly by the qadi, and the tax was apparently collected and paid to the Mongols. Presumably a similar levy had been imposed on Mosul. This tax resembles the capitation tax (*qubchūr*) that had been imposed some years before on Transoxiana, but was not to be systematically applied in western Asia for another six years. This incident strongly suggests that the Ayyubids readily acquiesced to Mongol domination, and shows how Lu'lu' served as their intermediary in relations with Syria.

46. An inscription on the Sinjār Gate (now destroyed) dated its reconstruction to 641. *RCEA*, 11:153 (no. 4229); van Berchem, "Monuments et inscriptions," 1:201–3.

47. Sibṭ, 493; al-Dhahabī, *Ta'rīkh al-Islām*, Bodl. MS Laud 305, f. 158a; Juvaynī, 2:507–8, 512. This levy was probably the result of the Governor Arghun's efforts to regularize the administration of Iran, Iraq, Rūm, and Syria, undertaken soon after his arrival in Khurasan in 641/1243–44. The tendency of this period, when the Mongols were founding their administrations in the conquered territories, was for occasional taxes to be replaced by fixed annual levies in areas of sedentary population. Curiously, the Damascus tax was levied in dirhems; accounts of similar taxes imposed elsewhere refer to dinars as the medium of payment. See Allsen, 147–49, 163–68; Schurmann, "Mongolian Tributary Practice," 310–12, 368–74; Lambton, "Mongol Fiscal Administration in Persia," 64:87–88; Vernadsky, *The Mongols and Russia*, 60, 140.

The subordination of the rulers of the region to Mongol authority is further revealed by their participation in the events surrounding the coronation of Güyük as Great Khan in Rabīʿ II 644/August 1246.[48] The rulers of Mosul, Aleppo, Baghdad, Rūm, and other cities of the region were summoned to send envoys to Mongolia to attend the coronation, and they travelled to Mongolia in the entourage of the governor Arghun. After the coronation, the envoy of al-Nāṣir of Aleppo was able to obtain from Güyük a *yarligh* (imperial edict) exempting al-Nāṣir and his dependents from taxation.[49] Güyük also named governors and commanders, confirming Arghun as governor of western Asia and naming the *noyan* Eljigidei to command the army in Rūm, Mosul, Syria, and Georgia.[50] Mosul may have established a permanent representative in Mongolia during this reign.[51]

Güyük's reign had little impact on western Asia, for the Khan was preoccupied with a feud that had arisen between his family and that of Batu, Khan of the Golden Horde. When Güyük died, in April 1248, Batu resumed his pressure on Mosul, the Jazīra, and Syria. In 649/1251 his *noyan* Baiju sent envoys to various kings of the region with edicts containing demands (*ḥawālāt*) for monetary

48. Juwaynī, 1:250; Rashīd al-Dīn, *Successors*, 180–83.

49. Ibn Shaddād, *Aʿlāq*, f. 41b; cf. Allsen, 20.

50. Ibn al-ʿIbrī, 256–57; Juvaynī, 1:257. Eljigidei was appointed to replace Chormaghun and his mission may have been to thwart Batu's efforts to extend his control into the Middle East any further. During Güyük's reign, the long-standing tension between the houses of Jochi and Tolui on one side, and Ögedei and Chaghadai on the other, nearly erupted into civil war. See Allsen, 19–21; Jackson, "Dissolution of the Mongol Empire," 198–202.

51. Rashīd al-Dīn, *Successors*, 191.

payments.[52] Al-Nāṣir and the rulers of Mosul, Rūm, Mārdīn, Mayyāfāriqīn, and Jazīrat b. ʿUmar were to pay two hundred thousand dinars each, and the ruler of Ḥiṣn Kayfā fifty thousand. Lu'lu' and the other rulers referred the envoys to Damascus, protesting that as dependents of al-Nāṣir they could not pay without his permission. Al-Nāṣir, after some dispute in his court, decided that the rulers could refuse payment on the basis of the exemption he had been granted by Güyük. He dismissed the Mongol envoys, who departed for Mosul accompanied by al-Nāṣir's envoy, Ibn Shaddād, who was sent along to explain to Lu'lu' and the other rulers that they need not pay the assessments. Ibn Shaddād gives a detailed account of his mission, which provides interesting insights into Lu'lu''s relationship with the Mongols.[53]

Lu'lu' met the Mongols in Ibn Shaddād's presence and informed them that he could not pay the assessments because he was a mamluk of al-Nāṣir and was thus exempted by Güyük's edict. The Mongols departed in anger, and then Lu'lu' turned to Ibn Shaddād and accused him of coming to Mosul to compromise him. Ibn Shaddād replied that the risk of arousing the Mongols would be borne by al-Nāṣir, not by Lu'lu'. This could have been of only scant comfort to Lu'lu', whose rule would undoubtedly have been swept away if the Mongols had sought revenge against al-Nāṣir. Lu'lu' summoned the resident Mongol agent (a *noyan*)[54] and

52. The anxiety Baiju's demands aroused in the courts of al-Nāṣir and Lu'lu' may be related to the uncertain outcome of the succession conflict then underway in Mongolia. On the succession and irregular Mongol demands see Allsen, 22–27, 67, 80, 146–47.

53. Ibn Shaddād, *Aʿlāq*, ff. 41a–42b. See the Appendix for a translation of this account.

54. On the duties of such resident agents see Allsen, 72–73.

complained about the demands. The agent reprimanded the envoys, apparently more for their behavior than for the demands as such. The agent then summoned Ibn Shaddād, who again repeated al-Nāṣir's refusal to pay assessments. The Mongol envoys now left Mosul. When they had crossed into the territory of Irbil, ruled by the Caliph, they were ambushed and massacred by Lu'lu''s troops. The Mongol resident agent sent for Lu'lu' and Ibn Shaddād and accused them of the atrocity. Lu'lu' denied responsibility, pointing out that the killing had not taken place in his territory, but promised in any case that he would seek to arrest those who had done it. Thereupon he took a group of condemned prisoners from his citadels, secluded them for awhile, and then brought them forth and executed them for the murder of the Mongols. The agent was satisfied. Lu'lu' told Ibn Shaddād confidentially that in al-Nāṣir's relations with the Mongols it would be best for him to follow Lu'lu''s example.

Ibn Shaddād's account clearly shows the risks Lu'lu' was prepared to run in order to please both his Mongol and his Ayyubid masters. Fortunately for Lu'lu', his treachery against the Mongols apparently went undiscovered, for the Mongols were poised to begin new conquests in the Middle East. In Rabīʿ II 649/July 1251 Möngke was enthroned as Great Khan. His elevation, secured with considerable help from his cousin Batu, represented the usurpation of the house of Ögedei, and was followed by a purge of all powerful members of the allied houses of Ögedei and Chaghadai. The newly united Mongol government began plans to secure and extend its conquests in the Middle East.

Undoubtedly Lu'lu' soon became aware of the change in Mongol policy, perhaps informed by his ambassador to Mongolia, whom Möngke had discharged with honor and sent home with a *yarligh* and *paiza* confirming Lu'lu''s rule.[55] Lu'lu' clearly wished to establish the closest possible ties to the Mongols. He continued his service as an intermediaty between the Mongols and the west, providing them with information and links to potentially sympathetic rulers.[56] In 652/1254 he sent his eldest surviving son al-Ṣāliḥ Ismāʿīl to Mongolia to represent him, and deposed a minister who refused to send his own son to Mongolia with him. He also took the dramatic step of replacing the Caliph's name with that of Möngke on Mosul's coins for 652.[57]

The Mongol Conquest

Möngke had entrusted the command of the renewed Mongol expansion in the west to his brother Hülegü, and exhaustive preparations were made to assemble the huge army and move it west. While an advance guard had entered northeastern Iran as early as March 1253 (Muḥarram 651),

55. Rashīd al-Dīn, *Successors*, 191. The *yarligh* was an imperial edict, probably concerning taxation or administrative matters. The *paiza* was a certificate conferring authority on its bearer. See Allsen, 70. Rashīd al-Dīn does not name any other rulers who received this honor, so it may be regarded as a singular distinction conferred on Lu'lu'.

56. The Ayyubid ruler al-Ashraf Mūsā, dispossessed of Ḥimṣ by al-Nāṣir, communicated with the Mongols secretly via Mosul in 651. See al-Yūnīnī, 2:310. Lu'lu' may also have kept the Mongols informed of noteworthy events in the west, such as the arrival of the Crusade of St. Louis in Egypt in Rabīʿ I 647/June 1249. See Pelliot, "Les Mongols et la Papauté," 8:[156–57].

57. Ibn Shaddād, *Aʿlāq*, f. 72b; idem, *Ẓāhir*, 115–16. Mosul's coins proclaim Möngke "Ruler of the World" (*khodāwandi ʿālam*) and Lu'lu' the "Sultan of Islam and the Muslims" (*sulṭān al-Islām waʾl-Muslimīn*). Lu'lu''s title suggests that he saw himself in a particularly distinguished role among the Muslim rulers of western Asia. See al-Ḥusaynī, 60, 123; Allsen, 43, 177–79.

Hülegü himself with the bulk of the army did not follow until December 1255 (Dhu'l-Qa'da 653). Perhaps disappointed by the glacial pace of the Mongol advance, Lu'lu' reinstated al-Nāṣir and the Caliph on Mosul's coins in 653.[58] Hülegü spent most of 654/1256 reducing the Ismā'īlī strongholds in Iran to submission.

Preparations for the conquest of Baghdad were begun in 655/1257 and launched in Dhu'l-Ḥijja/December, after the Caliph had rejected a series of demands for capitulation. Hülegü advanced via Kirmanshāh, Baiju from Anatolia via Mosul, and other commanders lead armies by way of Shahrazūr and Khūzistān. Lu'lu' was compelled to supply weapons, provisions, and war matériel, such as the bridge of boats over which Baiju's army crossed the Tigris in Muḥarram 656/January 1258.[59] Lu'lu''s son al-Ṣāliḥ Ismā'īl had returned to Mosul with Hülegü, and probably led a contingent of Mosul's troops in support of the Mongol attack.[60] The Mongol armies converged on Baghdad in the middle of Muḥarram/January and defeated the Caliph's army, which, ironically, was commanded by Lu'lu''s son-in-law al-Duwaydār al-Ṣaghīr. The Mongols breached the city wall on 28 Muḥarram 656/4 February 1258, and soon captured the city. The Caliph was executed on 14 Ṣafar/20 February. Hülegü returned to Adharbayjān in the spring and established a base at Maragha.

The Mongols seem to have found questionable aspects to Lu'lu''s conduct during the invasion, for there are

58. Edhem, 109; Hennequin, 260–61; al-Ḥusaynī, 124; Lane-Poole, 3:207.

59. Al-Makīn b. al-'Amīd, 166; Rashīd al-Dīn, *Histoire des Mongols*, 263; al-Dhahabī, *Ta'rīkh al-Islām*, Bodl. MS Laud 305, f. 248a; al-Ghassānī, 626; Ibn Wāṣil, Bibl. Nat. MS 1702, f. 127b; Ibn al-Ṭiqṭaqā, 65; Ibn Kathīr, 13:200.

60. Ibn al-'Ibrī, 276–77; Bar Hebraeus, 1:433–34; Ibn Wāṣil, Bibl. Nat. MS 1702, f. 385a.

several accounts of his being warned to remain loyal. One such account describes how the Mongols sent to Mosul the severed heads of three Baghdad leaders, including Lu'lu''s son-in-law al-Duwaydār al-Ṣaghīr, as an example to those who would resist their rule.[61] In another account, the Mongols criticized Lu'lu''s hesitation to send troops to support the Mongol force at Baghdad, an action that implied his loyalty depended on the outcome of the conflict.[62] Other accounts relate that Lu'lu' was in correspondence with the Caliph before the conquest, warning him of the need to arm himself in preparation for the invasion. Lu'lu''s letters were intercepted by the Caliph's wazir Ibn al-ʿAlqamī, who hoped to keep the Caliph in the dark about the true extent of the Mongol threat.[63] Some of these accounts link the Mongol suspicions to Lu'lu''s subsequent journey to Maragha to visit Hülegü, and describe how the aged Lu'lu' was able to persuade the victorious Mongol commander of his loyalty. Despite his advanced age—he was then more than eighty years old—Lu'lu' arrived in Maragha on 8 August 1258/6 Shaʿbān 656 to present Hülegü with gifts and reaffirm his submission to Mongol authority.[64] Hülegü confirmed him in his possessions and sent him back to Mosul.

Lu'lu''s visit to Maragha was more probably motivated by two factors: his desire to present himself in person

61. *Ḥawādith*, 328–29; Rashīd al-Dīn, *Histoire des Mongols*, 298–99; Baybars al-Manṣūrī, (Br. Libr.) ff. 31b–32a; al-Dhahabī, *Ta'rīkh al-Islām*, Bodl. MS Laud 305, f. 297b; Qirṭāy, ff. 56b–57a.

62. Ibn al-ʿIbrī, 276; Bar Hebraeus, 1:433–44.

63. Ibn Wāṣil, Bibl. Nat. MS 1703, f. 127b; al-Dhahabī, *Ta'rīkh al-Islām*, Bodl. MS Laud 305, f. 248a.

64. Ibn al-ʿIbrī, 276–77; Bar Hebraeus, 1:433–34; Ibn Wāṣil, 4:116; 5:50–51; Bibl. Nat. MS 1702, f. 386a; MS 1703, f. 140a; Rashīd al-Dīn, *Histoire des Mongols*, 319–23; al-Yūnīnī, 2:104; al-Dhahabī, *Ta'rīkh al-Islām*, Bodl. MS Laud 305, ff. 249b, 285b–86a, 306a.

to the representative of the authority who for so long had accorded him special status, and his wish to take possession of Irbil.[65] The Mongols had moved to occupy that city shortly after the fall of Baghdad, but its Kurdish garrison had seized control and would not submit to them, even when implored to do so by their governor, Ibn al-Ṣalāyā. The Mongols besieged the city, but its citadel was among the strongest in the region and the siege therefore became prolonged into the summer. Lu'lu' supplied troops and advice to the Mongols, and apparently purchased from them the right to undertake the siege on their behalf. Ibn Wāṣil reports that Lu'lu' slandered Ibn al-Ṣalāyā before Hülegü, causing the Mongols to execute the governor in Rabīʿ I or II of 656 (March–May 1258).[66] It seems more likely that Ibn al-Ṣalāyā's fate was linked with the rebellion of his city against the Mongols, but in either case, Lu'lu' was the principal beneficiary of his demise. He captured the city at the end of the summer.[67]

Lu'lu''s willingness to exploit the Mongols' displeasure with neighboring rulers is shown by his conduct at Amid in 655/1257. The Ayyubid ruler of Mayyāfāriqīn and Amid, al-Kāmil Muḥammad, had returned from Mongolia with Hülegü. When the Mongols ordered him to supply troops to aid in the conquest of Baghdad, al-Kāmil

65. The latter motive is suggested by the accounts of historians who assert that Lu'lu' persuaded Hülegü to execute Irbil's governor, Sharaf al-Dīn Ibn al-Salāyā.

66. Ibn Wāṣil, 5:50–51, Bibl. Nat. MS 1702, f. 386a; MS 1703, f. 140a; also in al-Dhahabī, *Ta'rīkh al-Islām*, Bodl. MS Laud 305, ff. 248a, 249b, 301a.

67. Al-Makīn b. al-ʿAmīd, 167; Bar Hebraeus, 1:430; Rashīd al-Dīn, *Histoire des Mongols*, 315–17. Lu'lu' did not long hold the city. His garrison appears to have been driven out by a Kurdish chief named Sharaf al-Dīn.

pleaded his inability to assemble a force of the size demanded. Hülegü responded by ordering him to be killed, but al-Kāmil eluded capture and fled back to Mayyāfāriqīn. When he reached that city, in Muḥarram 655/January–February 1257, he learned that one of his amirs, encouraged by Lu'lu', had rebelled and ruled Amid in Lu'lu''s name. Al-Kāmil succeeded in recapturing the city a few months later and nothing came of Lu'lu''s plot, but the incident serves to illustrate Lu'lu''s readiness to use Mongol power to extend his own domains.[68]

After the fall of Baghdad, Hülegü despatched a force, under his son Yoshmut, which besieged Amid and Mayyāfāriqīn in Dhu'l-Qa'da 656/November 1258. Lu'lu' sent a supporting force, commanded by his sons al-Ṣāliḥ Ismā'īl, al-Muẓaffar 'Alī, and al-Mujāhid Isḥāq, with engineers to build siege engines. Al-Kāmil attempted to end the siege through negotiation, but the talks were broken off when Lu'lu' informed the Mongols that al-Nāṣir Yūsuf, al-Kāmil's only possible liberator, was fully occupied suppressing a rebellion in his army in Syria. Because of this, Lu'lu''s old enemy, al-Sa'īd of Mārdīn, branded him a hypocrite (*munāfiq*)—although the justice of the remark is hard to understand when one considers that al-Sa'īd's own son was also supporting the Mongol siege. Mayyāfāriqīn eventually fell on 23 Rabī' II 657/19 April 1259, but Amid held out until the beginning of 659/1261.[69]

After the capture of Mayyāfāriqīn, Lu'lu''s son and heir al-Ṣāliḥ Isma'īl was summoned by Hülegü as he made his preparations for the conquest of Syria. Hülegü

68. Ibn Shaddād, *A'lāq*, ff. 73a, 79b; cf. Cahen, "Djazira," 121–22.

69. Ibn Shaddād, *A'lāq*, ff. 74a, 75a–b; Rashīd al-Dīn, *Histoire des Mongols*, 331, 363–75.

married al-Ṣāliḥ to Turkān Khātūn, a daughter of the Khwārazm Shāh Jalāl al-Dīn. She had been captured as a child when the Mongols defeated her father and raised at the Mongol court. The Mongols provided her with a dowry when she married, in accordance with their custom.[70] Shortly thereafter, Lu'lu' died, on Friday, 3 Sha'bān 657/26 July 1259, aged probably more than eighty years.[71] He had ruled Mosul in fact, if not in name, for more than forty years. His remains were buried first in Mosul's citadel, and were later transferred to the Madrasat al-Badriya immediately to the south. The Madrasa still stands, and is now a shrine to the Imām Yaḥyā Abu'l-Qāsim.

Domestic Policy

Before concluding this study with an account of the fall of Mosul, it is appropriate to consider the impact of Lu'lu''s reign on the city of Mosul itself. One can only be quite brief on this subject since there is little concrete evidence upon which to base generalizations. There are only two areas where Lu'lu''s actions may be related to particular social policies: his opposition to the Kurds, and his egalitarian treatment of Sunnīs and Shī'īs.

Lu'lu''s opposition to the Kurds, demonstrated dramatically during his rise to power, continued throughout

70. Juvaynī, 2:468; Bar Hebraeus, 1:426. Some accounts imply that the marriage occurred before the conquest of Baghdad. One account (Ibn Khaldūn, vol. 5, pt. 2, pp. 1151–52) reports that Hülegü sent al-Ṣāliḥ to Mongolia without telling Lu'lu'. He learned of al-Ṣāliḥ's whereabouts only when he sent his other sons to inquire.

71. The date is uncertain, for 26 July was a Saturday. See Ibn Khallikān, 1:184; Ibn Shaddād, *A'lāq*, f. 36b. Ibn al-'Ibrī (p. 279)/Bar Hebraeus (1:435) gives the date of 20 July (Monday).

his independent reign. In 644/1245 he executed Tāj al-ʿĀrifīn Shams al-Dīn, a Sufi shaykh and charismatic leader of the ʿAdawiya sect of the Kurds, for fear that the Kurds would rise in rebellion under his leadership.[72] A few years later, in 652/1254, the ʿAdawiya rebelled against excessive taxation, and were harshly repressed by Mosul's army. Lu'lu' ordered the execution of their leader and two hundred of his followers, and had the bones of Shaykh ʿAdī exhumed and burned.[73]

While zealous in his opposition to the Kurds, Lu'lu' was more tolerant than his Zangid predecessors in other respects. It is necessary to recount some history of the ulama in Mosul in order to see this aspect of Lu'lu''s policy in perspective.[74] Lu'lu''s master Arslān Shāh had been a notable patron of the Shāfiʿī *madhhab*; his reign was distinguished by their prominence in Mosul's civic affairs. They held the overwhelming majority of the city's key positions at court and in the judicial and educational establishments. Among the Shāfiʿīs of Arslān Shāh's time, the favored group consisted of families who had immigrated from provincial Zangid towns (most notably

72. Al-Dhahabī, *ʿIbar*, 5:183; idem, *Taʾrīkh al-Islām*, Bodl. MS Laud 305, f. 199b; al-Ṣafadī, *Al-Wāfī biʾl-wafayāt*, vol. 12, ed. Ramaḍān Abdel Tawwāb, Bibliotheca Islamica, vol. 61 (Wiesbaden: Franz Steiner Verlag, 1399/1979), 101–3; al-Ghassānī, 549. The ʿAdawiya sect was founded by Shaykh ʿAdī b. Musāfir, a Hakkārī Kurd. Over the years this sect, which was lead for some time by descendents of Shaykh ʿAdī, grew increasingly popular among the Kurds of the region. The ʿAdawiya eventually became the Yazīdīs, under which name they are known today. Shaykh ʿAdī's tomb at Lālish remains a shrine and center of pilgrimage for the Yazīdīs.

73. *Ḥawādith*, 271; al-Dhahabī, *Taʾrīkh al-Islām*, Bodl. MS Laud 305, ff. 243b–244a; al-Ghassānī, 601.

74. A fuller analysis is presented in the author's Ph.D. dissertation, "History of the Atabegs," 310–65.

the Ibn Muhājir, Ibn al-Athīr, and Ibn Man'a families). They had gradually acquired more and more prominent roles in Mosul's civic life. This group accorded more or less equal status to other Sunnī *madhhabs*, and they were comparatively tolerant of Mosul's large Christian community.[75] They had displaced an earlier Shāfi'ī clique, led by the enormous Shahrazūrī family, which had hitherto been dominant. The Shahrazūrīs' power was based in the office of qadi, which they had controlled since before the foundation of the Zangid dynasty (with only one brief interlude during Arslān Shāh's reign). Their fate was closely linked to that of the Zangids, stemming from their important role in securing the Saljuq Sultan's approval for 'Imād al-Dīn Zankī's rule over Mosul. Unlike the Shāfi'ī families of provincial origin, the Shahrazūrīs were decidedly intolerant of minority Sunnī sects.[76]

75. As examples, some taught in madrasas endowed half for Shāfi'īs and half for Ḥanafīs, the first such combined institutions in Islam. The Ibn Muhājir family endowed a madrasa for Shāfi'īs and a Dār al-Ḥadīth for Ḥanbalīs next door to it. Kamāl al-Dīn Ibn Man'a was known in Europe as well as the Middle East for his learning in the rational sciences, and he is said to have taught the Gospels and Torah to Christians and Jews (Ibn Khallikān, 5:311–18). Al-Dhahabī (*Ta'rīkh al-Islām*, Bodl. MS Laud 305, f. 306a) relates a tale about a lavish public celebration in Mosul on Palm Sunday, sponsored by Lu'lu' to rival Kūkburī's celebration in Irbil of the Prophet Muḥammad's birthday. If there is any truth to this fabulous story, it is that in Lu'lu''s Mosul Christians enjoyed more latitude than in most Muslim cities of the time. Since Christians probably formed a very large minority community in Mosul, this is not as remarkable as it seems. On the overall treatment of Christians in Mosul, see Fiey, *Mossoul chrétienne*, 39–46.

76. A revealing example is mentioned by al-Ṣafadi, *Al-Wāfī bi'l-wafayāt*, vol. 15, ed. Bernd Radtke, Bibliotheca Islamica, vol. 60 (Wiesbaden: Franz Steiner Verlag, 1399/1979), 331.

Despite their declining fortunes under Arslān Shāh and his successors, the Shahrazūrīs had retained their hold on the office of qadi. The break in their control seems to have occured in 630, when a member of the Ibn Muhājir family assumed the office.[77] Lu'lu''s suppression of the last of Mosul's Zangids a year later was probably not coincidental, for support from the ambitious emergent Shāfiʿī families would certainly have been an important factor in his success. Lu'lu''s association with these Shāfiʿī families is further evidenced by his employment of members of the Ibn Muhājir and Ibn al-Athīr families as envoys, and his patronage of the intellectual endeavors of ʿIzz al-Dīn Ibn al-Athīr and Kamāl al-Dīn Ibn Manʿa. Nevertheless, Shāfiʿī dominance in Mosul's affairs gradually declined during the latter half of Lu'lu''s rule, although there is no evidence that this was the consequence of a deliberate anti-Shāfiʿī policy on Lu'lu''s part.[78]

The equalization of status among the *madhhab*s and moderate Shīʿites is consistent with the *futuwwa* ethic that had been energetically promoted by the Caliph al-Nāṣir and his successor al-Mustanṣir.[79] That Lu'lu'

77. Al-Asnawī, 2:446.

78. This analysis is presented in somewhat greater deatil and with full biographical references in the author's dissertation. The decline in Mosul's Shāfiʿī population was steeper than the decline in ulama populations generally. The overall population of ulama in Mosul known from biographical dictionaries declined by two-thirds from peak numbers during the reign of Arslān Shāh. Of those who remained, the Shāfiʿīs comprised about fifty percent, a decline from about eighty percent in the time of Arslān Shāh and before. Members of the three principal Sunnī *madhhab*s and the ʿAlid house are mentioned in accounts of Lu'lu''s court and patronage. See Patton, "History of the Atabegs," 355–60 (and to the references cited there add Ibn al-Ṭiqṭaqā, 7, 100).

79. Hartmann, 92–135.

had adopted the *futuwwa* creed is apparent from the initiation of his sons into the order by notables of al-Mustanṣir's court. The burial of his daughter at the shrine of Kāẓimayn in Baghdad, in a funeral ceremony attended by Sunnī and 'Alid notables, also suggests the prevalence of *futuwwa* influence. The introduction of shrines dedicated to descendants of 'Alī into several of Mosul's Sunnī educational institutions, however, most clearly exemplifies the emerging acceptance of Shī'ism during Lu'lu''s reign. Shrines dedicated to the martyred descendants of 'Alī were built in the Badriya and 'Izziya Madrasas, and probably the Niẓāmiya, Nūriya, and other Madrasas as well.[80] An inscription[81] in the Badriya Madrasa (now the Mashhad of the Imām Yaḥyā Abu'l-Qāsim) dates the shrine to at least 637, or two years prior to the death of the madrasa's professor, the Shāfi'ī Kamāl al-Dīn Ibn Man'a. Other buildings in Mosul datable to Lu'lu''s reign contain inscriptions venerating the 'Alid martyrs. A final example of this type of policy is Lu'lu''s commissioning a Ḥanbalī scholar to write an account of the death of 'Alī. The scholar, who was said to have been an avid hater of Rafiḍī Shī'īs, "wrote what was true about the killing, without anything else."[82]

Such curious associations of Sunnīs and Shī'īs are a fascinating feature of this era, meriting fuller study from the vantage of the intellectual development of Islamic society. The adoption of a creed of mutual acceptance (for want of a more accurate phrase) between Sunnīs

80. See the numerous books and articles of Sa'īd al-Daywahjī, especially "Madāris al-Mawṣil fi'l-'ahd al-Atābakī."

81. *RCEA*, 11:120 (no. 4180).

82. He was 'Izz al-Dīn Abū Muḥammad 'Abd al-Razzāq b. Rizq Allāh al-Ras'anī (589–661/1193–1263). The work has apparently not survived. See al-Dhahabī, *Tadhkirat al-ḥuffāẓ*, 4:235–36.

and Shīʿīs throughout Iraq, but apparently not in Egypt and Syria, appears very significant to an understanding of the origin of sectarian differences between these regions.

Lu'lu''s policies, despite his firmness, were not without opposition. Muwaffaq al-Dīn al-Kawāshī,[83] an ascetic Shāfiʿī shaykh and author of an important commentary on the Qur'ān, refused to acknowledge Lu'lu' or stand in his presence. Al-Kawāshī spent the last forty years of his life within the confines of Mosul's vast Umayyad Mosque (long a stronghold of Mosul's conservative ulama). There, in the courtyard of the mosque, al-Kawāshī and his followers planted wheat purchased in the town of al-Jābiya in Syria, a conquest of the orthodox Caliph ʿUmar and the site of one of the *amṣār*, or settlement camps, founded by the conquering Arabs. They preferred to harvest and live upon this wheat rather than use local grain. The point of this protest is not explained in the sources, but it seems to hinge on the legitimacy of ʿUmar's rule, which would have been denied, or at least implicitly questioned, by a community accepting the legitimacy of Shīʿism.

83. Abu'l-ʿAbbās Aḥmad b. Yūsuf b. Ḥasan al-Shaybānī (590–680/1193–1281). See al-Dhahabī, *Ta'rīkh al-Islām*, Bodl. MS Laud 279, ff. 114b–15a (citing the historian Shams al-Dīn al-Jazarī, d. 739).

3

The Descendants of Lu'lu' and the Fall of Mosul

Lu'lu' attempted to pass on his legacy to his sons, but the turbulence generated by the Mongol occupation of Iraq was too great and they were soon swept away. The brief term of their rule was filled with dramatic events which vividly illuminate the tremendous instability of the region following Hülegü's invasion and Baybars' emergence as ruler of the Egyptian mamluks. It is impossible to say what sort of regime would have been established in Mosul had they survived, but the close relationship between Lu'lu''s descendants and the mamluks of Egypt suggests that two Mamluk dynasties might have evolved, one in Iraq and another in Egypt. There is little point to further speculation along these lines, and the following account is intended mainly to end the story of Badr al-Dīn Lu'lu' and his rule in Mosul at its natural conclusion: the fall of Mosul and the emigration of Lu'lu''s descendants to Egypt.

Lu'lu' had divided his realm among his sons before his death. His eldest surviving son, al-Ṣāliḥ Rukn al-Dīn Ismā'īl received Mosul, al-Mujāhid Sayf al-Dīn Isḥāq Jazīrat b. 'Umar, and al-Muẓaffar 'Alā' al-Dīn 'Alī Sinjār.[1] Mosul's coins verify the transfer of power in

1. Ibn Shaddād, *A'lāq*, ff. 25b, 27b; Ibn al-'Ibrī, 279; Bar Hebraeus, 1:435; Ibn Wāṣil, Bibl. Nat. MS 1702, ff. 391a–b; MS 1703, f. 145b.

Mosul, for some name Lu'lu' as ruler, others al-Ṣāliḥ.[2] The name of the Caliph usually found on Mosul's coins has been replaced (and sometimes overstamped) on all issues by the name of the Mongol Khan Möngke.

After his father's death, al-Muẓaffar ʿAlī abandoned his territories and fled to Syria to support al-Nāṣir Yūsuf, who was still trying to rally his forces to meet the Mongol invasion. Al-Ṣāliḥ occupied Sinjār in his absence and named his own son al-ʿĀdil Nūr al-Dīn Arslān Shāh as its governor. Qarqīsiyā was occupied by al-Nāṣir.[3] In Ramaḍān 657/September 1258 Hülegü left Adharbayjān and began his march toward Syria. He easily occupied most of the Jazīra, including Qarqīsiyā. He captured Naṣībīn (presumably a former territory of al-Muẓaffar ʿAlī) and presented it to al-Ṣāliḥ. Al-Ṣāliḥ seems to have been assigned to assist in the continuing Mongol siege at Amid.[4]

Hülegü's army occupied Syria, capturing Aleppo in Ṣafar 658/January 1260 and Damascus in Rabīʿ I/March. Al-Nāṣir fled south, where much of his remaining army, including Lu'lu''s son al-Muẓaffar ʿAlī,[5] abandoned him to join forces with the mamluks of Egypt. The Mongols soon captured al-Nāṣir and sent him to Hülegü, thereby ending independent Ayyubid rule in Syria. The consolidation of Mongol rule in Syria was prevented, however, by the emergence of tension in the Mongol ruling family

2. Artuk, 415; Hennequin, 263–65, 275–82.

3. Ibn Shaddād, *Aʿlāq*, ff. 25b, 37a. Ibn Wāṣil (Bibl. Nat. MS 1702, ff. 391a–b; MS 1703, f. 145b) says that Lu'lu' had sent ʿAlī to Syria. This seems unlikely, because ʿAlī had been present at the Mongol siege of Mayyāfāriqīn a few months before Lu'lu''s death. He had served al-Nāṣir in Syria earlier in the decade.

4. Ibn Shaddād, *Aʿlāq*, ff. 25b, 27b; Rashīd al-Dīn, *Histoire des Mongols*, 329–33.

5. Ibn Wāṣil, Bibl. Nat. MS 1702, ff. 391a–b; MS 1703, f. 145b.

following the death of the Khan Möngke on 19 Shaʿbān 657/11 August 1259.[6] Hülegü apparently anticipated aggression from his cousin Berke, Khan of the Golden Horde, and withdrew most of his forces from Iraq and Syria in order to meet it. He left only a token force in Syria under the command of his general Kitbuqa. The mamluks invaded Syria and defeated the Mongols in the famous battle at ʿAyn Jālūt in southern Palestine on 25 Ramaḍān 658/3 September 1260.[7] The mamluks quickly drove the Mongols from Syria and occupied the territory that had once belonged to al-Nāṣir. It is ironic that the mamluks' occupation of Syria was furthered by Hülegü, who executed their enemy al-Nāṣir when he learned of the Mongol defeat at ʿAyn Jālūt.

The mamluks were led by al-Muẓaffar Quṭuz, the successor of ʿIzz al-Dīn Aybak. When he reached Damascus in Shawwāl/September he appointed governors of the newly occupied territories; among them al-Muẓaffar ʿAlī b. Lu'lu', who received Aleppo.[8] ʿAlī was retitled al-Malik al-Saʿīd to avoid confusion with Quṭuz's own title. It is said that ʿAlī was chosen because of his ability to provide the mamluks with intelligence about Mongol activities in Iraq through his correspondence with his brother in Mosul. His appointment is said to have angered the mamluk general Baybars al-Bunduqdārī, who sought the governorship for himself, and may therefore have been a

6. Jackson argues that Berke's hostility toward Hülegü stemmed from the latter's usurpation of his family's traditional authority over western Asia. See "Dissolution," 208–27.

7. More was involved in the Mongols' defeat than the growing rivalry with Berke. See Smith, "ʿAyn Jālūt," 307–45; Morgan, 231–55.

8. Al-Makīn b. al-ʿAmīd, 176; Ibn ʿAbd al-Ẓāhir, 96; Ibn Wāṣil, Bib. Natl. MS 1703, ff. 162b–163a, 164b–166b; Baybars al-Manṣūrī, (Bodl.) ff. 176b–178a, (Br. Libr.) f. 42b; al-Yūnīnī, 1:374.

factor contributing to Baybars' assassination of Quṭuz on 15 Dhu'l-Qa'da 658/22 October 1260.

'Alī's governorship in Aleppo was extremely unsuccessful. He imposed excessive levies on the population and had great difficulty sustaining his authority over the mamluk commanders in his garrison. When a Mongol raiding party surprised and decimated one of his detachments, he was forced to lead all his forces toward the Euphrates to meet the Mongols. While camped east of Aleppo, his commanders learned of Quṭuz's assassination. They arrested 'Alī, who was able to save his life only by revealing the location of his private treasury. The Mongols attacked in force and reoccupied Aleppo in Dhu'l-Ḥijja 658/December 1260. 'Alī was released before their advance and fled toward Egypt, now ruled by Baybars. The Mongols were eventually stopped by a mamluk force near Ḥimṣ, but continued to hold Aleppo until April, when Baybars had established his authority over Syria and was able to dispatch an expedition to drive them out.

It is difficult to interpret Mongol activity in Iraq during this period. Hülegü held the bulk of the Mongol army in Adharbayjān, anticipating a confrontation with Berke. The Mongols remaining in Iraq were presumably engaged in efforts to preserve and consolidate their hold on the region. They ruled Mosul through Lu'lu''s son al-Ṣāliḥ Ismā'īl, who proclaimed his loyalty to Möngke on Mosul's coins of 657 through 659.[9] Mongol power may have been waning in Iraq, however, for al-Ṣāliḥ went to Syria in the early summer of 659/1261, apparently hoping to win mamluk support for the recovery of his territory.[10] He

9. Hennequin, 287–89; al-Ḥusaynī, 65; Lane-Poole, 9:306.

10. Bar Hebraeus (1:439–40, 442)/Ibn al-'Ibrī (pp. 282–83) dates his departure to May 1261 (Jumādā II 659); al-Yūnīnī (1:452–53) reports 10 Rajab/10 June. Ibn Shaddād (*A'lāq*, f. 37a) reports that he arrived in

clearly regarded the effort as something of a gamble, however, for he took his money and dependents, and was accompanied by many other citizens of Mosul. Bar Hebraeus reports that the reason he left was that the Mongols had intercepted a message to him from his brother 'Alī in Egypt, which urged him to revolt and support Baybars. The message fell into the hands of the Christian governor of Mosul's Nineveh district, Shams al-Dīn Muḥammad Ibn Yūnus al-Ba'shīqī, who sent it to the Mongols in the hope of ending al-Ṣāliḥ's harassment of the Christians of his district and his confiscation of their properties.

Al-Ṣāliḥ first went to Qarqīsiyā, and wrote to his brother al-Mujāhid Isḥāq in Jazīrat b. 'Umar urging him to abandon his territories as well. He then continued on to Egypt while al-Mujāhid made preparations to leave Jazīra. When the Mongol governor of Jazīra learned that al-Mujāhid was preparing to flee, he tried to arrest him, but was prevented from doing so by the residents of the city. Al-Mujāhid then extorted money from the Christians in his territories and departed for Egypt. Both rulers arrived in Cairo within a few days of each other, and were received with great pomp by Baybars. Baybars gave al-Ṣāliḥ money, clothes, and a house outside the Bāb al-Qanṭara; al-Mujāhid also received a house; their retainers were granted salaries. Al-Ṣāliḥ was accompanied by his son 'Alā' al-Mulk (sometimes called 'Alā' al-Dīn) and al-Mujāhid came with his sons Ḥusām al-Dīn Birka Khān

---

Egypt on 12 Rajab/12 June; Ibn 'Abd al-Ẓāhir (pp. 114–16) gives the month as Sha'bān/July. Al-Yūnīnī notes that al-Mujāhid arrived in Egypt on 2 Ramaḍān/31 July, a few days after his brother. Other accounts of the exodus are Abū Shāma, 212–13; Ibn Wāṣil, Bibl. Nat. MS 1702, ff. 397a–b; *Ḥawādith*, 344–45; Rashīd al-Dīn, *Histoire des Mongols*, 380–81; al-Dhahabī, *Ta'rīkh al-Islām*, Bodl. MS Laud 305, f. 256b.

and Jalāl al-Dīn Muḥammad. Another son of Lu'lu' came with them, al-Kāmil Nāṣir al-Dīn Muḥammad.[11] Other refugees from Iraq reached Egypt at about the same time, among them a man named Aḥmad b. al-Ẓāhir who was able to prove that he was member of the 'Abbāsid family. He was accordingly proclaimed Caliph under the name al-Mustanṣir Billah on 17 Rajab 659/17 June 1261.[12]

The arrival of Iraqi refugees in Egypt during the spring and summer of 659/1261 corresponds to a time of Mongol weakness in Iraq. Hülegü was perhaps mustering his forces for war against the Golden Horde, and had left Iraq too thinly defended. No sizeable Mongol army appears to have been left in Iraq following their loss of Aleppo in the spring of 659/1261. The Mongol force that attempted to arrest al-Mujāhid at Jazīrat b. 'Umar was easily driven off by a band of citizens.[13] The Mongols were also unable to prevent a renegade mamluk commander, Shams al-Dīn Aqwash al-Barlī, from establishing his authority over Ḥarrān and other towns of the western Jazīra during the summer.[14]

The Mongols' waning power did not escape the notice of Baybars. By the end of summer, he had fully established his control over Syria, although he still had trouble holding Aleppo. To further consolidate his power, he had the new Caliph invest him as Sulṭān on 19 Ramaḍān/17 August. Baybars then led his army into Syria, accompanied by the sons of Lu'lu'. Baybars had a dual purpose: he wanted to end the threat posed to Aleppo

11. Ibn Shaddād, *Ẓāhir*, 331–32.

12. Ibn 'Abd al-Ẓāhir, 111–12.

13. Bar Hebraeus, 1:442.

14. Ibn Shaddād, *A'lāq*, f. 11b; Ibn Wāṣil, Bibl. Nat. MS 1702, ff. 396a–b; Baybars al-Manṣūrī, (Bodl.) ff. 178b–80b; al-Yūnīnī, 2:105–6, 109, 118–22, 152.

by the renegade commander al-Barlī; and he wanted to send the new Caliph and the sons of Lu'lu' into Iraq to recover their lands from the Mongols.[15] Toward these ends, in Dhu'l-Qa'da/October, he sent one group of his army to the north with orders to pursue al-Barlī and also stand ready to assist the Caliph if needed; another group accompanied the Caliph and the sons of Lu'lu' along the Euphrates toward Baghdad.

The Caliph's expedition to recover Baghdad is one of the more puzzling incidents among the many events of this very complicated period of history. Baybars' defenders claimed that he spent more than a million dinars equipping the Caliph and his force; his detractors fault him for leaving the Caliph helpless before the Mongol garrison at Baghdad. The balance of the argument seems to favor Baybars. Mongol forces in Iraq were undeniably weak; they had been defeated by minor forces at least twice since the sons of Lu'lu' fled to Egypt. Baybars' hopes for the recovery of Baghdad may have been bolstered by the evident dissension between Hülegü and his cousin Berke, Khan of the Golden Horde. In slightly more than a year hence, Berke and Hülegü would fight a battle over the control of Adharbayjān. The presence of the sons of Lu'lu' on the expedition is evidence of the optimism then prevelant in mamluk circles. It is unlikely that the Iraqis would have returned to their territories in the face of certain defeat and death at the Mongols' hands. The recovery of Iraq seemed so probable that even the renegade mamluk commander al-Barlī had sent an expedition toward Baghdad led by his own candidate for Caliph, an 'Abbāsid who had taken the title al-Ḥākim.

15. Abū Shāma, 213; Ibn Shaddād, *A'lāq*, f. 37a; Ibn 'Abd al-Ẓāhir, 76, 111–12; Ibn Wāṣil, Bib. Nat. MS 1702, ff. 395b–396a; Baybars al-Manṣūrī, (Br. Libr.) ff. 48a–b; al-Yūnīnī, 2:108–9.

The expedition of both Caliphs, however, was doomed.[16] Leading fewer than a thousand men, al-Mustanṣir occupied a few towns along the Euphrates without opposition. At al-Raḥba the sons of Lu'lu' left him to go directly to their own territories, asserting that they had had no instructions from Baybars to stay with him the whole way. About sixty of their father's mamluks elected to remain with the Caliph. While on the march, they were joined by some Arab bands and a few troops sent by the ruler of Ḥamāh. At Ṣiffīn, al-Barlī's contender for the Caliphate joined forces with al-Mustanṣir and contributed another six or seven hundred men. But when they reached Anbār on 3 Muḥarram 660/28 November 1261, the Mongol garrison of Baghdad met and annihilated them in a close, hard-fought battle. Al-Mustanṣir disappeared, the manner of his death never to be known; al-Ḥākim escaped and reached Cairo, where Baybars installed him as Caliph in succession to al-Mustanṣir.

After leaving the Caliph, the sons of Lu'lu' went to Sinjār. Al-Ṣāliḥ wrote to Mosul to find out about conditions there, and was urged to return as soon as possible. Much had happened since his departure six months previously.[17] His wife Turkān Khātūn, a Khwārazmian captive raised at the Mongol court, had seized control of Mosul with the support of its garrison commander, a man named Yāsān. She closed the city to a group of mamluks who had accompanied al-Ṣāliḥ part way to Syria and then turned

16. Bar Hebraeus, 1:442–43; Ibn 'Abd al-Ẓāhir, 116; Ibn Wāṣil, Bibl. Nat. MS 1702, f. 396a; Qirṭāy, ff. 76a–b; al-Yūnīnī, 2:109, 156; Ibn al-Dawādārī, 8:82; al-Dhahabī, *Ta'rīkh al-Islām*, Bodl. MS Laud 305, ff. 258a, 324a; Ibn Kathīr, 13:233, 235; al-Maqrīzī, vol. 1, pt. 2, pp. 462–63.

17. Ibn al-'Ibrī, 283–84; Bar Hebraeus, 1:440–41; *Ḥawādith*, 344–45; Rashīd al-Dīn, *Histoire des Mongols*, 381; al-Yūnīnī, 2:156.

back. While they camped outside the city seeking to gain admission, the head of the city's civil administration, a state secretary (*kātib al-inshā'*) named Muḥyī al-Dīn Ibn Zablāq, led a successful popular revolt. Supported by the people of Mosul's Shahr Sūq quarter, he captured the Bāb al-Jisr and admitted al-Ṣāliḥ's mamluks. Turkān Khātūn and her supporters retreated to the citadel. The rebels took control of the city and embarked on a devastating persecution of the Christian population, who were doubtless suspected of being in sympathy with the Mongols. A Mongol force now approached to take control of the town, and the city mamluks went out to drive them off. The Mongols defeated them and killed them to the last man, and presumably then camped outside the city in preparation for siege. Nothing is known about the situation between the two parties in the city, or of the activities of the Mongols outside. Mosul is said to have had about four hundred defenders. Presumably the small Mongol force simply blockaded the city pending the availability of forces capable of undertaking a siege.

Encouraged by Mosul's defenders, and also probably knowing that the Caliph's army was then still advancing unopposed toward Baghdad, al-Ṣāliḥ left his brothers behind at Sinjār and went to Mosul. His force, which numbered only about three hundred men, killed the Mongol governor at Naṣībīn and, on 20 Dhu'l-Ḥijja 659/15 November 1261, easily slipped into Mosul through the small Mongol force that encircled the city.[18] Al-Ṣāliḥ publicly

18. Accounts of the siege and fall of Mosul are Abū Shāma, 218–19; Ibn Shaddād, *A'lāq*, ff. 11b, 37a–b; Ibn al-'Ibrī, 283–84; Bar Hebraeus, 1:441–43; Ibn 'Abd al-Ẓāhir, 116; *Ḥawādith*, 346–47; Qirṭāy, f. 78b; Rashīd al-Dīn, *Histoire des Mongols*, 381–89; Baybars al-Manṣūrī (Br. Libr.) f. 49b; al-Yūnīnī, 1:492–95, 2:152, 156–69, 164; al-Dhahabī, *Ta'rīkh al-Islām*, Bodl. MS Laud 305, ff. 258a, 324b.

proclaimed his defiance of Mongol authority by issuing coins dated 659 bearing the names of the Caliph al-Mustanṣir and Baybars.[19] But the timing of his return could not have been worse: a few days later a large Mongol force, under the general Sandāghū, arrived at Mosul to commence siege operations. They erected two dozen mangonels to hammer the city's walls, and completely isolated the already starved city from further provisions or reinforcements. Al-Ṣāliḥ's only hope was to bring in a large relieving force from Syria. His brothers left Sinjār when they heard of the defeat of the Caliph and returned to Egypt to ask Baybars for help. Al-Ṣāliḥ wrote to al-Barlī, the nearest mamluk commander with any strength, and asked him for aid. Meanwhile, al-Ṣāliḥ determined to hold out as long as he could. It was some time before Baybars and al-Barlī responded to the appeals. Al-Barlī led a small force of fourteen hundred men to Sinjār, but he was intercepted and easily defeated by a larger Mongol force on 14 Jumādā II 660/6 May 1262. Al-Barlī's power was broken by this defeat, which forced him to submit to Baybars' authority. Baybars' army had left Egypt in Jumādā I, but since it spent a month just to reach Damascus, it is questionable whether he sincerely intended to relieve Mosul. An alternative motive for Baybars' slowness is suggested by the fact that when the Egyptians heard of al-Barlī's defeat, they moved immediately to occupy his lands in northern Syria and abandoned the Mosul expedition altogether.

The Mongols sent captured members of al-Barlī's army into Mosul to convince its defenders that further resistance was hopeless. Having no further hope for relief, al-Ṣāliḥ opened negotiations concerning Mosul's

19. Artuq, 415–16; Edhem, 114; Hennequin, 289–91; al-Ḥusaynī, 66.

surrender. Much discussion apparently centered on clemency for his three-year-old son 'Alā' al-Mulk, who was innocent of complicity in his father's resistance. It is possible that al-Ṣāliḥ hoped the Mongols would retain his son as ruler of Mosul, for they had done as much once before when they captured Mārdīn.[20] At the beginning of Sha'bān/June al-Ṣāliḥ turned his son over to the Mongols, believing that they would send him to Hülegü. Next the Mongols demanded that al-Ṣāliḥ give himself up, threatening to massacre the city's inhabitants if he did not. The Mongols are said to have promised al-Ṣāliḥ that he would be sent to Hülegü with a recommendation that he be treated leniently. Al-Ṣāliḥ vacillated, but was eventually persuaded by his exhausted supporters to accept, and he left Mosul after prayer on Friday, 15 Sha'bān 660/5 July 1262.[21]

The Mongols now controlled the city, but they did not immediately enter it. First they sent in a Christian—Shams al-Dīn al-Ba'shīqī, the former governor of the Nineveh district—with a decree proclaiming that the citizens would be spared any mistreatment. Commerce then resumed for a time while the Mongols razed the city wall. Then, on 26 Sha'bān 660/16 July 1262, the Mongols entered the city in force and began extensive looting and killing. They are said to have executed 'Alā' al-Mulk and hung his body in two pieces at the Bāb al-Jisr. They sent al-Ṣāliḥ toward Hülegü's camp near Lake Van, and executed him either en route or soon after he arrived.[22] Lu'lu''s

20. The Mongols besieged Mārdīn, held by the Artuqid ruler al-Sa'īd. When they captured it, they conferred it on al-Sa'īd's son al-Malik al-Muẓaffar, who continued to serve the Mongols loyally and was present with his forces in the Mongol camp at the siege of Mosul.

21. The date is uncertain, for 5 July was a Wednesday.

22. Gruesome accounts are related about the manner of his execution. See Rashīd al-Dīn, *Histoire des Mongols*, 389–91.

son al-Kāmil Muḥammad and the state secretary Ibn Zablāq were also killed. The Mongols named al-Ba'shīqī Governor of Mosul, the first of several Christian governors of the city under early Mongol rule. When Sandāghū finished with his operations at Mosul, he went to Jazīrat b. 'Umar, and besieged and captured it in the summer of 661/1263. Thus ended the rule of Lu'lu''s sons over northern Iraq.

Although the reassertion of Mongol authority in Iraq had ended the rule of Lu'lu''s sons, they did not immediately give up all hope. Al-Mujāhid Isḥāq and al-Muẓaffar 'Alī found refuge in Egypt and were welcomed by Baybars in Muḥarram 660/December 1261.[23] Baybars gave Isḥāq a hundred thousand dirhems and each brother received lands in the Fayyūm and the command of a hundred horsemen. Al-Muẓaffar 'Alī built a public bath near his house on the bank of Cairo's Canal (al-Khalīj).[24] The sisters, children, and mamluks of the sons of Lu'lu' also received *iqṭā'* or salaries.[25] On 23 Muḥarram one of their sisters married Bīlīk al-Khizandār, one of the leading officers of Baybars' state, in the Maydān al-Aswād below the Cairo citadel. The betrothal had occurred the preceding fall during Baybars' march toward Syria with the Caliph and the sons of Lu'lu'.[26]

In 661/1263 Isḥāq corresponded with one of his mamluks still in Jazīrat b. 'Umar, whom the Mongols had

23. Ibn 'Abd al-Ẓāhir, 116; Qirṭāy, ff. 78b–79a; al-Yūnīnī, 1:495, 2:156; al-Dhahabī, *Ta'rīkh al-Islām*, Bodl. MS Laud 305, f. 258a; Ibn Kathīr, 13:234.

24. Ibn Shaddād, *Ẓāhir*, 360–61.

25. Among the refugees was Mujāhid al-Dīn Qāymāz, the mamluk commander of the expedition sent by Lu'lu' to aid al-Nāṣir against the Egyptians in 648–49. He sold a group of mamluks to the future Egyptian sultan Qalā'ūn, among whom was Baybars al-Manṣūrī, author of a history much used herein. See Baybars al-Manṣūrī (Bodl.), f. 49b.

26. Ibn 'Abd al-Ẓāhir, 86–87; al-Yūnīnī, 1:453, 483, 2:107–8; Ibn Kathīr, 13:233.

named governor of the town, in an effort to recover some money he had left behind. The mamluk was prepared to comply, but one of his servants took the money instead to a mamluk of Lu'lu''s still in 'Imādiya. Lu'lu''s mamluk told the Mongols, who had Isḥāq's mamluk executed. A Christian was named governor in his place.[27]

No more conspiracies or contacts with the east are recorded. Hereafter, the sons of Lu'lu' are mentioned only occasionally in connection with the activities and ceremonies of the Mamluk court. In 662/1264 a son of Isḥāq, among several other sons of the leading figures of Baybars' court, was circumcised in a grand ceremony along with the Sultan's son al-Sa'īd.[28] In 663/1265, Baybars reconquered large portions of Palestine which had long been held by the Crusaders, and divided the occupied lands among a large number of dispossessed amirs and retainers. 'Alī and Isḥāq each received half the *iqṭā'* of a village called Dannāba, while their brother-in-law Bīlīk received half the *iqṭā'* of the nearby village of Ṭūr Karam.[29] In 664/1266 Isḥāq was with Baybars' army at the siege of Safad, where he told the historian Ibn 'Abd al-Ẓāhir about Baybars' extraordinary efforts in bringing a large mangonel to the site of the siege.[30] Later in the campaign, after the fall of the Crusader fort Shaqīf (Beaufort) in Rajab 666/April 1268, Baybars gave ceremonial robes to "his kings," among whom were the sons of Lu'lu'.[31] In 672/1273, when Baybars went to meet a feared

27. Bar Hebraeus, 1:443–44.
28. Ibn 'Abd al-Ẓāhir, 213–14.
29. Qirṭāy, ff. 80b–81a; al-Yūnīnī, 2:318; Ibn al-Dawādārī, 8:111–12; Mufaḍḍal (ed. Blochet), 483. The villages are known today as Dhannāba and Ṭūl Karm.
30. Ibn 'Abd al-Ẓāhir, 257.
31. Ibn 'Abd al-Ẓāhir, 298.

Mongol invasion which never materialized, he was accompanied from Yaffa to Damascus by the "son of the Lord of Mosul."[32]

For their many actions in service of Baybars, the sons of Lu'lu' expected the Sultan to assert their claims to rule in the east. Their hopes remained unfulfilled at Baybars death in 676/1277, and their fortunes declined considerably under his successors.[33] Their relative Bīlīk did not long outlive Baybars, and his loss could only have further undermined their influence at court. Nevertheless they did survive, and apparently persisted in their claims. In 1282 the Khan Aḥmad, a successor of Hülegü who ruled 680–83/1281–84, sent peace overtures to the Mamluks. The Sultan al-Manṣūr Qalā'ūn sought to impose the condition that Mosul be ruled by the sons of Lu'lu'.[34] Nothing came of these negotiations, for Aḥmad was soon deposed, but they serve to indicate the durability of the pretensions of Mosul's émigré monarchs.

It is not known when 'Alī and Isḥāq died. Three of Isḥāq's sons are known, and at least two survived into the 8th/14th century. Jalāl al-Dīn Muḥammad b. Isḥāq died in 720/1320–21.[35] Quṭb al-Dīn Ibrāhīm and 'Alā' al-Dīn were pupils of an important Ḥanbalī *muḥaddith*, Najīb al-Dīn al-'Amidī (587–672), who taught at the Madrasat al-Kamāliya in Cairo.[36] 'Alā' al-Dīn, who lived 657–731/1259–1331, was said to have been a soldier (*jundī*).[37] These three are the last known descendants of Badr al-Dīn Lu'lu'.

32. Ibn Shaddād, *Ẓāhir*, 73; Mufaḍḍal (ed. Blochet), 382.
33. Ibn Wāṣil, Bibl. Nat. MS 1702, f. 397b.
34. Bar Hebraeus, 1:467–69.
35. Mufaḍḍal (ed. Kortantamer), 13.
36. Al-Dhahabī, *Ta'rīkh al-Islām*, Bodl. MS Laud 279, ff. 72b–73a.
37. Ibn al-Wardī, 2:420; al-Maqrīzī, vol. 2, pt. 1, p. 339.

APPENDIX

Ibn Shaddād's Diplomatic Mission to Mosul in 649

From Ibn Shaddād, *Al-A'lāq al-khaṭīra fī dhikr umarā' al-Shām wa'l-Jazīra*, Berlin, Staatsbibliothek Preussischer Kulturbesitz, Orient-abteilung, MS Sprenger 199 (Ahlwardt no. 9800), ff. 41a–43a.

Account of the Death of Mu'izz al-Dīn Maḥmūd and the Rule of his Son al-Malik al-Mas'ūd Shāhanshāh.

Al-Malik al-Mu'aẓẓam Mu'izz al-Dīn Maḥmūd b. Mu'izz al-Dīn Sanjarshāh b. Sayf al-Dīn Ghāzī b. Quṭb al-Dīn Mawdūd b. 'Imād al-Dīn Zankī b. Aq Sunqur, Lord of al-Jazīra, died at the end of 648. The cause of his death was that he was a glutton and ate too much one day. He got indigestion from it, and he lingered a few days with it and died by the grace of God. After him his son al-Malik al-Mas'ūd Shāhanshāh ruled Jazīrat b. 'Umar and continued in it.

The year 649

Al-Malik al-Nāṣir Ṣalāḥ al-Dīn Yūsuf b. al-Malik al-'Azīz, Lord of Syria, had returned from his defeat by the Egyptians at al-Manṣū[r]a. When he reached Damascus—and with him was al-Malik al-Muẓaffar 'Alā' al-Dīn

ʿAlī b. Badr al-Dīn Luʾluʾ Lord of Mosul and Mujāhid al-Dīn Qāymāz, Muqaddim ʿAskar of Mosul, who had joined him at al-ʿArīsh when he attacked Egypt—envoys of Badr al-Dīn Luʾluʾ Lord of Mosul came to him twenty days after his arrival with fine gifts of horses, cloth, and articles equal to twenty thousand dinars to congratulate him on his safety. With them was a letter to his [Luʾluʾ's] son al-Malik al-Muẓaffar ʿAlāʾ al-Dīn ʿAlī aforesaid, in which he ordered him to continue to serve the *Mawla* al-Malik al-Nāṣir, "and if he plunges into the sea, plunge with him, and if he goes into fire, go with him."

A few days later envoys of Baiju *Noyan* arrived with merchants, and they had edicts (*yaghāligh*) containing claims (*ḥawālāt*) on all the kings, namely on the Sultan al-Malik al-Nāṣir for 200,000 dinars, on the lord of Rūm ʿIzz al-Dīn for 200,000, on Badr al-Dīn Luʾluʾ Lord of Mosul for 200,000, on al-Malik al-Saʿīd Lord of Mārdīn for 200,000, on al-Malik al-Kāmil Lord of Mayyāfāriqīn [*f. 41b*] for 200,000, on the Lord of al-Jazīra for 200,000, and on the Lord of Ḥiṣn Kayfā for 50,000. The envoys and merchants had gone to all the kings and stated what was in the edicts, and they referred them to us. They pleaded that "Sultan al-Malik al-Nāṣir is our chief, and we make the *khuṭba* for him. We cannot pay what he does not pay."

So they came to al-Malik al-Nāṣir as we have mentioned and they asked him. Al-Zayn Sulaymān al-Ḥāfiẓ[1] and

1. Zayn al-Dīn Sulaymān b. ʿAlī Ibn al-Muʾayyad al-Ḥāfiẓī (d. 662) was a prominent figure in the court of al-Nāṣir. He collaborated with the Mongols during their invasion of Iraq and joined Hülegü's entourage after the Mongol conquest of Syria. His *nisba* stems from his early career as a physician to al-Malik al-Ḥāfiẓ, an Ayyubid prince of Jaʿbar. See al-Dhahabī, *ʿIbar*, 5:267–68; al-Ṣafadī, 15:414–15; Ibn al-ʿImād, 5:308–9; al-Kububī, 2:77–78.

others advised him to appease them. The compiler of this book said: "I say why should we appease them? When Tāj al-Mulūk went to Güyük Khan in 643 they wrote edicts for him, the contents of which were that we neither accept claims nor support the [Mongol] army (*lā naqbal ḥawāla wa-lā nanjud bi-ʿaskar*)." When the king heard my speech, he sent to Aleppo and asked that the edicts be brought. When they arrived, he found their contents as I said. He directed me to go with the envoys to the aforesaid kings to arouse their anger (*li-'uḥāniquhum*) in the presence of the envoys and merchants, and he ordered me to set off.

At this time envoys of al-Malik al-Masʿūd Lord of al-Jazīra arrived calling for help from al-Malik al-Sulṭān [*sic*] al-Nāṣir against Badr al-Dīn Lu'lu' Lord of Mosul and complaining about him and his transgressions against him at the time of the death of his father al-Malik al-Muʿaẓẓam. He asked to submit al-Jazīra to him [al-Malik al-Nāṣir] and be compensated for it. Al-Malik al-Nāṣir at that time could not, because of his preoccupation with the Egyptians, take al-Jazīra and compensate for it, so he authorized me to mediate for him about it with Badr al-Dīn Lu'lu' Lord of Mosul, and reconcile the two of them. He sent with me the customary horses, robes, and a banner, and I set out.

The envoys preceded me to Mosul. Majd al-Dīn ʿAbd al-Raḥman Ibn al-Ṣāḥib Kamāl al-Dīn ʿUmar known as Ibn al-ʿAdīm[2] had gone to Mosul to console him [Lu'lu'] for

2. The Ibn al-ʿAdīm family was a prominent Ḥanafī ulama family in Aleppo. Kamāl al-Dīn Abu'l-Qāsim ʿUmar b. Aḥmad b. Hibat Allāh Ibn Abī Jarāda Ibn al-ʿAdīm al-Ḥawāzanī al-ʿUqaylī al-Ḥalabi (588–660) was a qadi of Aleppo and a prominent scholar and historian. His history of Aleppo is an important source for the history of this era. His son Majd al-Din Abu'l-Majd ʿAbd al-Raḥman (d. 677) was a qāḍī al-quḍāh and lived in Damascus and Aleppo. Among the many biographical notices on Kamāl

[the loss of] his son, and so he preceded me to it. When I reached Mosul, I met Badr al-Dīn Lu'lu' Lord of Mosul and I conveyed the messages I had. I spoke with him about the problem of al-Malik al-Mas'ūd, and mediated on his behalf for the Sultan al-Malik al-Nāṣir. He began to relate what al-Malik al-Mas'ūd had done to him after the death of his father, such as committing acts of aggression and making his daughter hear foul language. He mentioned what is not proper. Then he ordered me to be where I could hear his daughter's speech, but I refused and said "proof is unnecessary with the word of the Sultan; his word is sufficient." [*f. 42a*]

He said to me: "The land is fit for one who is useful to the Muslims and treats them well; but this one [al-Mas'ūd] is occupied by his devotion to pleasures, eating and drinking. When a calamity befalls the Muslims, he is useless. I will convey to the Sultan al-Malik al-Nāṣir 50,000 dinars cash if he will turn over al-Jazīra to me. You stay with me until I send [an envoy] to him and ask his advice."

But I did not believe him, and I said: "It is not proper for you to refuse the robe of al-Malik al-Nāṣir and his standard." When he could not induce me to agree with him about what he wanted, he broke off discussions with me and spoke with Majd al-Dīn Ibn al-'Adīm [instead]. He [Majd al-Dīn] wrote a letter to his son [*sic*] Kamāl al-Dīn and to the Sultan al-Malik al-Nāṣir,

---

al-Dīn are al-Dhahabī, *'Ibar*, 5:261; al-Qurashī, 1:386–87; al-Ṣafadī, *Al-Wāfī bi'l-wafayāt*, vol. 22, ed. Ramzī Baalbakī, Bibliotheca Islamica, vol. 6v (Wiesbaden: Franz Steiner Verlag, 1404/1983), 421–26; Ibn al-'Imād, 5:303; al-Kutubī, 3:126–29; B. Lewis, "Ibn al-'Adīm," *EI*2 3 (1968): 695–96; *GAL*, 1:332. On Majd al-Dīn see al-Dhahabī, *'Ibar*, 5:315; Ibn al-'Imād, 5:358; al-Qurashī, 1:303; al-Yūnīnī, 3:306–20.

saying to him that "someone has asked Badr al-Dīn to leave your authority on account of the Lord of al-Jazīra." The Sultan al-Malik al-Raḥīm Badr al-Dīn Lu'lu' settled with the Ṣāḥib Kamāl al-Dīn secretly about that to which al-Malik al-Nāṣir was disposed. He sent him envoys alarming him about me, and he sent an envoy with me to the Lord of al-Jazīra.

I left him and went to al-Jazīra. When the envoy of Badr al-Dīn arrived [in Damascus], he sent him secretly to the Sultan al-Malik al-Nāṣir, and he met with the Ṣāḥib Kamāl al-Dīn, and Shaykh Najm al-Dīn al-Bādarā'ī[3] of the Dīwān. The two of them and al-Malik al-Muẓaffar 'Alā' al-Dīn 'Alī b. Badr al-Dīn Lu'lu' agreed, and they persisted until they took the kerchief (*mandīl*)[4] of the Sultan al-Malik al-Nāṣir that, when his course was clear on the Egyptian front, he would permit him to take it.

When I arrived at al-Jazīra, al-Malik al-Mas'ūd clung to me and said: "I will turn al-Jazīra over to you and go to al-Malik al-Nāṣir. You remain [here]." I refused this and left al-Jazīra to go to Mārdīn.

We return to what happened between Badr al-Dīn Lord of Mosul and the Tatar envoys who arrived with claims: When the envoys who were mentioned before reached Badr al-Dīn,

3. Najm al-Dīn Abū Muḥammad 'Abd Allāh b. Abu'l-Wafā' Muḥammad b. al-Ḥasan al-Bādarā'ī al-Baghdādī al-Shāfi'ī a-Faraḍi (594–655) was a prominent and successful envoy of the Caliph, often named in accounts of diplomatic negotiations. His name derives from the district of Bādarāyā, southest of Baghdad. See al-Ṣafadī, *Al-Wāfī bi'l-wafayāt*, vol. 17, ed. Dorothea Krawulsky, Bibliotheca Islamica, vol. 6q (Wiesbaden: Franz Steiner Verlag, 1401/1982), 580–81; al-Subkī, 8:159; al-Dhahabī, *Ta'rīkh al-Islām*, Bodl. MS Laud 305, ff. 280b–281a; *Ḥawādith*, 322–23.

4. I have been unable to locate any other reference to this practice. The "kerchief" appears to represent the Sultan's permission.

he summoned me and them. They claimed from him 100,000 dinars. His reply was that "I am a mamluk of the Sultan al-Malik al-Nāṣir, and his deputy in the land. I make the *khuṭba* for him, and the land is his land. If he agrees with you about paying, I will pay." My reply was that: "I said we have edicts exempting us, whose contents are that we not accept demands and not support the army." So they left Badr al-Dīn and they spoke to him in an unseemly manner. [*f. 42b*]

He said to me: "You came with them only so that they would be irritated by me." So I said to him: "You are the cause of his [al-Nāṣir's] boldness, which should worry neither you nor us." These words convinced him to break with them. Their departure from his court was most shameless. Then he summoned the deputy of the Tatar in Mosul, who was called a *Noyan*, and complained to him about them. He summoned them and reprimanded them. Then he sent them to me—I was in the Lion House (*Dār al-Sabu'*) in Mosul—and my reply to the envoys was: "We will pay you nothing, and we do not accept the claims because the edicts which we have require this. None of these kings who follow us will pay you anything." They left Mosul complaining about me and about Badr al-Dīn.

They left the territory of Mosul and entered the land of Irbil. Badr al-Dīn secretly sent a company to intercept them and kill them to the last one, and they took the cloth and goods that they had. When the *Noyan* heard about this, he summoned me in the presence of Badr al-Dīn and scolded him for this. He said: "They were not killed in my land, but I will search for whoever did this thing." He secretly ordered them to assemble from all the citadels those who were going to be executed and to conceal them for a time. Among them were some in irons. He ordered them all hung, and he turned the clothes over to the *Noyan* and said: "these are the ones who attacked the envoys, and this is what they took from them." This pleased the *Noyan* and satisfied him.

Then Badr al-Dīn Lu'lu' said to me privately: "I think in this matter our master the Sultan al-Malik al-Nāṣir had best do likewise."

Account of Badr al-Dīn Lu'lu' Ruling al-Jazīra.

It was said before that the Sultan al-Malik al-Nāṣir gave his kerchief to Shaykh al-Bādarā'ī and al-Malik al-Muẓaffar 'Alā' al-Dīn 'Alī, son of Badr al-Dīn Lu'lu' Lord of Mosul, on the preceding conditions, which were that when he was free of his preoccupation with Egypt, he would permit Badr al-Dīn to take al-Jazīra. When the kerchief reached him, he did not adhere to the conditions, but went to it, invested it, and besieged it until he took it in Rajab 649. He seized al-Malik al-Mas'ūd, made him get in a boat (*zawraq*), and sent him toward Mosul. It was the last knowledge about him. He was the last who remained of the Atabeg House. The term of their rule was 157 years from when the father of 'Imād al-Dīn Zankī ruled until this al-Malik al-Mas'ūd was drowned. Praise be to Him whose rule alone persists!

When Badr al-Dīn ruled it, he bestowed it on his son al-Malik al-Mujāhid Sayf al-Dīn Isḥāq. It remained in his control as deputy to his father until Badr al-Dīn died in Sha'bān 657. His son al-Malik al-Mujāhid became independent in it [*f. 43a*] and it remained in his control until the Tatar ruled Syria. His brother al-Malik al-Ṣāliḥ acquired a fear of the enemy which made him leave Mosul, which he had ruled after his father, and take refuge in Egypt. He remained there in the service of the kings of Egypt, until we compiled this book in 679.

Al-Jazīra reverted to Tatar rule, and their deputies are in it until when we compiled this book, which is 679.

Account of the Lands Controlled by al-Malik al-Nāṣir in the Jazīra.

The lands he controlled in the Jazīra were: Ḥarrān, al-Ruhā, Sarūj, al-Raqqa, Qala'at Ja'bar, al-Bīra, Jamalīn, al-Muwazzar; in Diyār Rabī'a: Naṣībīn, Ra's al-'Ayn, Dārā, the Khābūr in its entirety, and Qarqīsiyā, excepting Sinjār, Balad, and Jazīrat b. 'Umar.

BIBLIOGRAPHY

Abel, F.-M. "La liste des donations de Baîbars en Palestine d'après la charte de 663 H. (1265)." *Journal of the Palestine Oriental Society* 19 (1939–40): 38–44.

Abū Shāma al-Maqdisī, *Tarājim al-rijāl al-qarnayn al-sādis wa'l-sābi'*, known as *Al-Dhayl 'ala'l-rawḍatayn*. Edited by Muḥammad Zāhid Ibn al-Ḥasan al-Kawtharī. Cairo: Maktab Nashrat al-Thiqafat al-Islāmiya, 1366/1947.

Abu'l-Fidā, *Kitāb al-mukhtaṣar fī akhbār al-bashar*. 7 vols. Beirut: Dār al-Biḥār, 1375–81/1956–61.

Ahlwardt, W. *Die Handschriften-Verzeichnisse der Königlichen Bibliothek zu Berlin*. Vols. 7–9, 16–22, *Der Arabischen Handschriften*. 10 vols. Berlin, 1887–99.

Allsen, Thomas T. *Mongol Imperialism*. Berkeley: University of California Press, 1987.

Amedroz, H. F. "Three Arabic MSS. on the History of the City of Mayyāfāriqīn." *Journal of the Royal Asiatic Society* 34 (1902): 785–812.

Amitai, Reuven. "Mongol Raids into Palestine (A.D. 1260 and 1300)." *Journal of the Royal Asiatic Society*, 1987, 236–55.

Artuk, İbrahim and Cevriye Artuk. *İstanbul Arkeoloji Müzeleri Teşhirdeki İslâmî Sikkeler Kataloğu*. İstanbul: Milli Eğitim Basımevi, 1970.

Al-Asnawī. *Ṭabaqāt al-shāfi'iya*. Edited by 'Abd Allāh al-Jibūrī al-Baghdādī. 2 vols. Baghdad: n.p., 1390–91/1970–71.

Ayalon, David. "Aspects of the Mamlūk Phenomenon." *Der Islam* 53 (1976): 196–225; 54 (1977): 1–32.

———. "Le régiment bahriya dans l'armée mamelouke." *Revue des études islamiques*, 1951, 133–41.

Bar Hebraeus. *The Chronography of Gregory Abû'l Faraj*. Translated by Ernest A. Wallis Budge. 2 vols. London: Oxford University Press, 1932. (See also under Ibn al-'Ibrī, the author's Arabic name.)

Baybars al-Manṣūrī. *Zubdat al-fikra fī ta'rīkh al-hijra*. Oxford, Bodleian Library, MS Pococke 324; London, British Library, MS Add. 23,325.

Al-Birzālī. *Ta'rīkh Miṣr wa-Dimashq*. Berlin, Staatsbibliothek Preussischer Kulturbesitz, Orientabteilung, MS Sprenger 61 (Ahlwardt no. 9449).

Boyle, John Andrew. "The Death of the Last 'Abbasid Caliph: A Contemporary Muslim Account." *Journal of Semitic Studies* 6 (1961): 145–61.

———. "Dynastic and Political History of the Īl-Khāns." In *The Saljuq and Mongol Periods*, edited by J. A. Boyle, 303–421. Vol. 5 of *The Cambridge History of Iran*. Cambridge: Cambridge University Press, 1968.

Cahen, Claude. "La chronique de Ḳirṭāy et les francs de Syrie." *Journal asiatique* 229 (1937): 140–45.

———. "La «Chronique des Ayyoubides» d'al-Makīn b. al-Amīd." *Bulletin d'études orientales* 15 (1955–57): 108–84.

———. "La correspondance de Ḍiyā ad-Dîn ibn al-Athīr." *Bulletin of the School of Oriental and African Studies* 14 (1952): 34–43.

———. "La Djazira au milieu du treizième siècle d'après 'Izz-ad Din Ibn Chaddad." *Revue des études islamiques* 8 (1934): 109–28.

———. "Futuwwa." *EI²* 2 (1965): 961–65.

———. "Lu'lu'." *EI²* 5 (1983): 821.

———. "The Mongols and the Near East." In *The Later Crusades, 1189–1311*, edited by Robert Lee Wolff and Harry W. Hazard, 715–34. Vol. 2 of *A History of the Crusades*. Edited by Kenneth M. Setton. 4 vols. Madison: University of Wisconsin Press, 1969–77.

———. *Pre-Ottoman Turkey*. Translated by J. Jones-Williams. New York: Taplinger Publishing Company, 1968.

———. "Une source pour l'histoire des croisades: les mémoires de Sa'd ad-Dîn Ibn Hamawiya Juwaïnî." *Bulletin de la Faculté des lettres de Strasbourg* 28 (1930): 320–37.

Combe, Étienne, Jean Sauvaget, and Gaston Wiet, eds. *Répertoire chronologique d'épigraphie arabe*. 16 vols. Cairo: Institut français d'archéologie orientale, 1931–64.

Al-Daywahjī, Sa'īd. *Jawāmi' al-Mawṣil fī mukhtalif al-'uṣūr*. Baghdad: Maṭba'at Shafīq, 1382/1963.

———. "Madāris al-Mawṣil fī'l-'ahd al-Atābakī." *Sumer* 13 (1957): 101–18.

———, ed. *Manhal al-awliyā' wa-masrab al-aṣfiyā' min sādāt al-Mawṣil al-ḥadbā'*, by Muḥammad Amīn b. Khayr Allāh al-Khaṭīb al-'Umarī. 2 vols. Mosul: Maṭba'at al-Jumhūriya, 1385–88/1967–68.

———. "Mashhad al-imām Yaḥyā b. al-Qāsim." *Sumer* 24 (1968): 171–82.

———. *Al-Mawṣil fi'l-'ahd al-Atābikī*. Baghdad, 1378/1958.

———, ed. *Munyat al-udabā' fī ta'rīkh al-Mawṣil al-ḥadbā'*, by Yāsīn b. Khayr Allāh al-Khaṭīb al-'Umarī. Mosul: Maṭba'at al-Hadaf, 1374/1955.

———, ed. *Tarjamat al-awliyā' fi'l-Mawṣil al-ḥadbā'*, by Aḥmad Ibn al-Khayyāṭ al-Mawṣilī. Mosul: Maṭba'at al-Jumhūriya, 1385/1966.

Al-Dhahabī. *'Ibar fī khabar man ghabar*. Edited by Ṣalāḥ al-Dīn al-Munjid and Fu'ād al-Sayyid. 5 vols. Kuwait: Maṭba'at Ḥukūma, 1960–66.

———. *Kitāb duwal al-Islām*. 2nd ed., 2 vols. Hyderabad: Osmania Oriental Publications, 1364–65/[1944–46].

———. *Kitāb tadhkirat al-ḥuffāẓ*. 4 vols. Hyderabad: Dā'irat al-Ma'ārif al-Niẓāmiya, 1333–34/[1914–16].

———. *Ta'rīkh al-Islām wa-wafayāt al-mashāhir wa'l-a'lām*. Vol. 18, pt. 1. Edited by Bashshār 'Awwād Ma'rūf. Cairo: 'Īsā al-Bābī al-Ḥalabī, 1397/1977. Manuscripts: London, British Library, MS Or. 52; Oxford, Bodleian Library, MSS Laud 279 and 305; Paris, Bibliothèque nationale, MS 1582.

D'Ohsson, G. *Histoire des Mongols*. 4 vols. The Hague: Les Frères van Cleef, 1834–35.

Doudou, Boulaid. "Der Tārīḫ al-Manṣūrī des Ibn Naẓīf al-Ḥamawī." Ph.D. diss., Universität Wien, 1961.

Edhem, I. Ghalib. *Catalogue des monnaies turcomanes. Musée impérial ottoman*. N.p., 1894. Reprint. Bologna: Arnaldo Forni Editore, n.d.

Farès, Bishr. "L'art sacré chez un primitif musulman." *Bulletin de l'Institut français d'archéologie orientale* 36 (1953–54): 619–77.

Fiey, J. M. *Mossoul chrétienne*. Beirut: Imprimerie catholique, 1959.

Al-Ghassānī, *Al-'Asjad al-masbūk wa'l-jawhar al-maḥkūk fī ṭabaqāt al-khulāfā' wa'l-mulūk*. Edited by Shākir Maḥmūd 'Abd al-Mun'im. Baghdad: Dār al-Bayān, 1395/1975.

Gibb, Hamilton A. R. "The Aiyūbids." In *The Later Crusades, 1189–1311*, edited by Robert Lee Wolff and Harry W. Hazard, 693–714. Vol. 2 of *A History of the Crusades*. Edited by Kenneth M. Setton. 4 vols. Madison: University of Wisconsin Press, 1969–77.

Glidden, H. W. Review of *Epigrafika vostoka* (Oriental Epigraphy), vols. 1–8, edited by V. A. Krachkovskaya. *Ars Orientalis* 2 (1957): 547–50. (Includes reviews of articles by I. Y. Kratchkovski, V. A. Kratchkovskaya, and L. T. Gyuzalyan listed elsewhere in this bibliography.)

Gottschalk, Hans L. "Die ägyptische Sultanin Šağarat ad-Durr in Geschichte und Dichtung." *Wiener Zeitschrift für die Kunde des Morganlandes* 61 (1967): 41–61.

———. *Al-Malik al-Kāmil von Egypten und seine Zeit*. Wiesbaden: Otto Harrassowitz, 1958.

Grousset, René. *The Empire of the Steppes*. Translated by Naomi Walford. New Brunswick: Rutgers University Press, 1970.

Gyuzalyan, L. T. "Nadpis' s imenem Badr al-dīna Lūlū na bronzovom podsvechnike Gosudarstvennogo Ermitazha" (Inscriptions with the name of Badr al-Din Lu'lu' on a bronze chandelier of the Hermitage). *Epigrafika vostoka* 2 (1948): 76–82.

Hartmann, Angelika. *Al-Nāṣir li-Dīn Allāh (1180–1225)*. Studien zur Sprache, Geschichte und Kultur des Islamischen Orients, edited by Bertold Spuler, n.f. 8. Berlin: Walter de Gruyter, 1975.

Al-Ḥawādith al-Jāmiʿa wa'l-tajārib al-nāfiʿa fi'l-mā'i al-sābiʿa. Edited by Muṣṭafā Jawād. Baghdad: Maṭbaʿat al-Furāt, 1351/[1932–33]. (When published, this manuscript was attributed to Ibn al-Fuwaṭī, but that identification has been questioned. See F. Rosenthal, "Ibn al-Fuwaṭī," *EI*2 3 (1968): 769.)

Hennequin, Gilles. *Catalogue des monnaies musulmanes de la Bibliothèque nationale*. Paris: Bibliothèque nationale, 1985.

Holt, P. M. *The Age of the Crusades*. London: Longman, 1986.

———. "Some Observations on the ʿAbbāsid Caliphate of Cairo." *Bulletin of the School of Oriental and African Studies* 47 (1984): 501–7.

Howorth, Henry H. *History of the Mongols*. 4 vols. London: Longmans, Green, and Co., 1876–1927.

Humphreys, R. Stephen. "The Emergence of the Mamluk Army." *Studia Islamica* 45 (1977): 67–99, 147–82.

———. *From Saladin to the Mongols*. Albany: State University of New York Press, 1977.

Ḥusayn, Muḥsin Muḥammad. *Irbil fi'l-ʿahd al-Atābikī*. Baghdad: Maṭbaʿat Asʿad, 1976.

Al-Ḥusaynī, Muḥammad Bāqir. *Al-ʿUmlat al-Islāmiya fi'l-ʿahd al-Atābikī*. Baghdad: Maṭbaʿat Dār al-Jāḥiẓ, 1386/1966.

Ibn ʿAbd al-Ẓāhir. *Al-Rawḍ al-zāhir fī sīrat al-Malik al-Ẓāhir*. Edited by ʿAbd al-ʿAzīz al-Khuwayṭir. Riyadh: n.p., 1396/1976.
Ibn Abiʾl-Damm. *Kitāb al-shamārīḥ fiʾl-tawārīkh*. Oxford, Bodleian Library, MS Marsh 60.
Ibn al-ʿAdīm. *Zubdat al-ḥalab min taʾrīkh Ḥalab*. Edited by Sāmī al-Dahhān. 3 vols. Damascus: Institut français de Damas, 1370–87/1951–68.
Ibn al-Athīr, Ḍiyāʾ al-Dīn. *Tarassul*. London, School of Oriental and African Studies, MS 47,281; Oxford, Bodleian Library, MS Pococke 322.
Ibn al-Athīr, ʿIzz al-Dīn. *Al-Kāmil fiʾl-taʾrīkh*. Edited by C. J. Tornberg. 12 vols. Leiden: E. J. Brill, 1851–71. Reprint. Beirut: Dar Sader, 1385/1965.
———. *Taʾrīkh al-bāhir fiʾl-dawlat al-Atābikiya*. Edited by A. A. Tolaymat. Cairo: Dār al-Ḥadīth, 1382/1963.
Ibn al-Dawādārī. *Al-Durra al-zakiya fī akhbār dawlat al-mulūk al-turkiya*. Edited by Ulrich Haarmann. Vol. 8 of *Kanz al-durar wa-jāmiʿ al-ghurar*. Deutsches Archäologisches Institut Kairo, Quellen zur Geschichte des Islamischen Ägyptens, vol. 1h. Cairo: ʿĪsā al-Bābī al-Ḥalabī, 1391/1971.
Ibn al-Fuwaṭī. *Al-Ḥawādith al-Jāmiʿa waʾl-tajārib al-nāfiʿa fiʾl-miʾa al-sābiʿa*. (See entry under title above.)
———. *Talkhīṣ majmaʿ al-adāb fī muʿjam al-alqāb*. Vol. 4. Edited by Muṣṭafā Jawād. 4, 4 parts. Damascus: Maṭbūʿāt Mudīriya Iḥyāʾ al-Turāth al-Qadīm, 1962–67.
Ibn al-ʿIbrī. *Taʾrīkh mukhtaṣar al-duwal*. Edited by Anṭūn Ṣāliḥānī al-Īsūʿī. N.p., 1890. Reprint. Beirut: Maṭbaʿat al-Kāthūlīkiya, 1958. (See also under Bar Hebraeus, the author's Syriac name.)
Ibn al-ʿImād al-Ḥanbalī. *Shadharāt al-dhahab fī akhbār man dhahab*. 8 vols. Cairo: Maktabat al-Qudsī, 1350–51/[1931–32].
Ibn al-Mustawfī. *Taʾrīkh Irbil*. Dublin, Chester Beatty Library, MS 4098.
Ibn al-Sāʿī. *Al-Jāmiʿ al-mukhtaṣar fī ʿunwān al-tawārīkh wa-ʿuyūn al-siyar*. Edited by Mustafa Djawâd and Père Anastase-Marie de St. Elie. Baghdad: Imprimerie syrienne catholique, 1353/1934.
[———. *Al-Muʿallim al-Atābikī*.] Berlin, Staatsbibliothek Preussischer Kulturbesitz, Orientabteilung, MS Sprenger 52 (Ahlwardt no. 9776). (On the attribution of this work to Ibn al-Sāʿī, see Douglas Patton, "Ibn al-Sāʿī's Account of the Last of the Zangids," *Zeitschrift der Deutschen Morgenländischen Gesellschaft* 138 (1988): 148–58.)

Ibn al-Ṭiqtaqā. *Al-Fakhrī fi'l-ādāb al-sulṭāniya wa'l-duwal al-Islāmiya*. Edited by Hartwig Derenbourg. Bibliothèque de l'Ecole des haute études, vol. 105. Paris: Librairie Émile Bouillon, Editeur, 1895.

Ibn al-Wardī. *Tatimmat al-mukhtaṣar fī akhbār al-bashar*. Edited by Aḥmad Rif'at al-Badrāwī. 2 vols. Beirut: Dār al-Ma'rifa, 1389/1970.

Ibn Bāṭīsh. "An Edition of the Ghāyat al-Wasā'il ilā Ma'rifat al-awā'il by Ismā'īl b. Hibat Allāh al-Mawṣilī known as Ibn Bāṭīsh (575–655/1179–1257)." Edited by 'Abd al-'Azīz b. Nāṣir al-Mānī'. Ph.D. diss., University of Exeter, 1976.

Ibn Bībī. *Die Seltschukengeschichte des Ibn Bībī*. Translated by Herbert W. Duda. Copenhagen: Ejnar Munksgaard, 1959.

Ibn Kathīr. *Al-Bidāya wa'l-nihāya fi'l-ta'rīkh*. 14 vols. Cairo: Maṭba'at al-Sa'āda, 1358/[1940].

Ibn Khaldūn. *Kitāb al-'ibar*. Edited by Y. A. Dāghir. 7 vols. Beirut: Dār al-Kitāb al-Lubnānī, 1956–59.

Ibn Khallikān. *Wafayāt al-a'yān wa-anbā' abnā' al-zamān*. Edited by Iḥsān 'Abbās. 8 vols. Beirut: Dār Ṣādr, 1968.

Ibn Naẓīf al-Ḥamawī. *Al-Ta'rīkh al-Manṣūrī, talkhīṣ al-kashf wa'l-bayān fī ḥawādith al-zamān*. Facsimile edition by P. Gryaznevitch. Moscow: Institute of the Peoples of Asia, 1960.

Ibn Shaddād. *Al-A'lāq al-khaṭīra fī dhikr umarā' al-Shām wa'l-Jazīra*. Berlin, Staatsbibliothek Preussischer Kulturbesitz, Orient-abteilung, MS Sprenger 199 (Ahlwardt no. 9800).

———. *Ta'rīkh al-Malik al-Ẓāhir* (Die Geschichte des Sultans Baibars). Edited by Aḥmad Ḥuṭayṭ. Bibliotheca Islamica, no. 31. Wiesbaden: Franz Steiner Verlag, 1304/1983.

Ibn Taghribirdī. *Al-Nujūm al-zāhira fī mulūk Miṣr wa'l-Qāhira*. Edited by Aḥmad Zakī al-'Adawī. 10 vols. Cairo: Maṭba'at Dār al-Kutub al-Miṣriya, 1348–68/1929–49.

Ibn Wāṣil. *Mufarrij al-kurūb fī akhbār banī Ayyūb*. Edited by Jamāl al-Dīn al-Shayyāl, Ḥasanayn Muḥammad Rabī', and Sa'īd 'Abd al-Fatāḥ 'Āshūr. 5 vols. Cairo: Maṭba'at Dār al-Kutub, 1960–72. Manuscripts: Paris, Bibliothèque nationale, MSS 1702 and 1703.

Irwin, Robert. *The Middle East in the Middle Ages: the Early Mamluk Sultanate 1250–1382*. London: Croom Helm, 1986.

Jackson, P. "The Dissolution of the Mongol Empire." *Central Asiatic Journal* 22 (1978): 186–244.

Al-Jalabī, Dā'ūd. "Al-Malik Badr al-Dīn Lu'lu' wa'l-āthār al-qadīma al-Islāmiya fi'l-Mawṣil." *Sumer* 2, no. 1 (1946): 20–28.

James, David. "An Early Mosul Metalworker: Some New Information." *Oriental Art* n.s. 26 (1980): 318–21.

Juvaynī. *The History of the World-Conquerer*. Translated by John Andrew Boyle. 2 vols. Manchester: Manchester University Press, 1958.

Khowaiter, Abdul-Aziz. *Baibars the First: his Endeavours and Achievements*. London: Green Mountain Press, 1978.

Kratchkovskaya, V. A. "Nadpis' bronzovogo taza Badr al-dīna Lūlū" (Inscription on a bronze basin of Badr al-Dīn Lu'lu'). *Epigrafika vostoka* 1 (1947): 9–22.

Kratchkovski, I. Y. "Ob odnom epitete v nadpisi bronzogo taza Lūlū" (On an epithet in the inscription of Lu'lu''s bronze basin). *Epigrafika vostoka* 2 (1948): 3–8.

Krehl, Ludolf. "Ueber einige muḥammadanische Münzen des Königlichen Münz-Cabinets zu Dresden." *Zeitschrift der Deutschen Morgenländischen Gesellschaft* 12 (1858): 250–63.

Kritzeck, James. "Ibn-al-Ṭiqṭaqa and the Fall of Baghdād." In *The World of Islam, Studies in Honor of Philip K. Hitti*, edited by James Kritzeck and R. Bayly Winder, 159–84. London: Macmillan, 1959.

Al-Kutubī, Ibn Shākir. *Fawāt al-wafayāt*. Edited by Iḥsān 'Abbās. 5 vols. Beirut: Dār Ṣādr, 1973–74.

Lambton, A. K. S. "Mongol Fiscal Administration in Persia." *Studia Islamica* 64 (1986): 79–99; 65 (1987): 97–123.

Lane-Poole, Stanley. *Catalogue of Oriental Coins in the British Museum*. 10 vols. London: Trustees of the British Museum, 1875–90.

Le Strange, G. "The Story of the Death of the Last Abbasid Caliph, from the Vatican MS. of Ibn-al-Furāt." *Journal of the Royal Asiatic Society*, 1900, 293–300.

Al-Mānī', 'Abd al-'Azīz b. Nāṣir. "An Edition of Ghāyat al-Wasā'il ilā ma'rifat al-awā'il by Ismā'il b. Hibat Allāh al-Mawṣilī known as Ibn Bāṭīsh (575–655/1179–1257)." Ph.D. diss. University of Exeter, 1976.

Al-Maqrīzī. *Kitāb al-sulūk li-ma'rifat duwal al-mulūk.* Edited by Muḥammad Muṣṭafā Ziyāda and Sa'īd 'Abd al-Fatāḥ 'Āshūr. 4 vols. Cairo: Maṭba'at Dār al-Kutub al-Miṣriya, 1352–92/1934–73.

Margoliouth, D. S. "On the 'Royal Correspondence' of Diya'-eddin Eljazari," *Actes du dixième Congrès international des orientalistes, session de Genève*. Part 3, section 3 (1894): 9–21.

Mason, Herbert. *Two Statesmen of Mediaeval Islam*. The Hague: Mouton and Co., 1972.

Morgan, David O. "The Mongols in Syria 1260–1300." In *Crusade and Settlement*, edited by Peter W. Edbury, 231–35. Cardiff: University College Cardiff Press, 1985.

Mufaḍḍal Ibn Abu'l-Faḍā'il. *Al-Nahj al-sadīd wa'l-durr al farīd fīmā ba'd ta'rīkh Ibn al-'Amīd*. Edited and translated by E. Blochet. *Patrologia Orientalis* 12 [1915]: 343–550; 14 (1920): 375–672; 20 (1928): 1–270.

———. *Al-Nahj al-sadīd wa'l-durr al farīd fīmā ba'd ta'rīkh Ibn al-'Amīd*. Edited and translated by Samira Kortantamer. *Ägypten und Syrien zwischen 1317 und 1341 in der Chronik des Mufaḍḍal b. Abī l-Faḍā'il*. Islamkundliche Untersuchungen, vol. 23. Freiburg im Breisgau: Klaus Schwarz Verlag, 1973.

Al-Mundhirī. *Al-Takmila li-wafayāt al-naqala*. Edited by Bashār 'Awwād Ma'rūf. 6 vols. Vols. 1–4, Najaf: al-Adab Press, 1388–91/1968–71. Vols. 5–6, Cairo: 'Īsā al-Bābī al-Ḥalabī, 1395–96/1975–76. Manuscript: London, British Library, MS or. 1541.

Al-Nasawī. *Sīrat al-Sulṭān Jalāl al-Dīn Mankubirtī*. Edited by Ḥāfiẓ Aḥmad Ḥamdī. Cairo: Dār al-Fikr al-'Arabī, 1953.

Patton, Douglas. "Badr al-Dīn Lu'lu' and the Establishment of a Mamluk Government in Mosul." *Studia Islamica*, in press.

———. "A History of the Atabegs of Mosul and their Relations with the Ulama, A.H. 521–660/A.D. 1127–1262." Ph.D. diss., New York University, 1982.

———. "Ibn al-Sā'ī's Account of the Last of the Zangids." *Zeitschrift der Deutschen Morgenländischen Gesellschaft* 138 (1988): 148–58.

Pelliot, Paul. *Les Mongols et la Papauté*. Extrait de la *Revue de l'Orient Chrétien*. 3rd ser., 3 (1922–23): 3–30; 4 (1924): 225–335; 8 (1931–32): 3–84. Paris: Librairie Auguste Picard, 1923–31.

Qirṭāy al-'Izzī al-Khizandārī. *Ta'rīkh al-nawādir mimmā li'l-awā'il wa'l-awākhir*. Gotha, Landesbibliothek, MS Orient. A 1655.

Al-Qurashi. *Al-Jawāhir al-muḍīya fī ṭabaqāt al-ḥanafīya*. 2 vols. Hyderabad: Dā'irat al-Ma'ārif al-Niẓāmiya, 1332/1913.

Rashīd al-Dīn. *Histoire des Mongols de la Perse*. Edited and translated by Étienne Quatremère. Paris, 1836. Reprint. Amsterdam: Oriental Press, 1968.

———. *The Successors of Genghis Khan*. Translated by John Andrew Boyle. New York: Columbia University Press, 1971.

Rice, D. S. "The Aghānī Miniatures and Religious Painting in Islam." *The Burlington Magazine* 95 (April 1953): 128–34.

———. "The Brasses of Badr al-Dīn Lu'lu'." *Bulletin of the School of Oriental and African Studies* 13 (1950): 627–34.

———. "Inlaid Brasses from the Workshop of Aḥmad al-Dhakī al-Mawṣilī." *Ars Orientalis* 2 (1957): 283–326.

———. "The Oldest Dated 'Mosul' Candlestick A.D. 1225." *The Burlington Magazine* 91 (December 1949): 334–40.

———. "Studies in Islamic Metal Work - II." *Bulletin of the School of Oriental and African Studies* 15 (1958): 61–79.

Richards, D. S. "Ibn al-Athīr and the Later Parts of the *Kāmil*: A Study of Aims and Methods." In *Medieval Historical Writing in the Christian and Islamic Worlds*, edited by D. O. Morgan, 76–108. London: School of Oriental and African Studies, 1982.

Runciman, Steven. *A History of the Crusades*. 3 vols. Cambridge: Cambridge University Press, 1951–54. Reprint. New York: Harper and Row, 1964–67.

Al-Ruwayshidī, Sawādī. *Imārat al-Mawṣil fī 'ahd Badr al-Dīn Lu'lu'*. Baghdad: Maṭba'at al-Irshād, 1971.

Saare, Friedrich and Ernst Herzfeld. *Archäeologische Reise im Euphrat- und Tigris-Gebiet*. 4 vols. Berlin: D. Reimer, 1911–20.

Saare, Friedrich and Max van Berchem. "Das Metallbecken des Atabeks Lulu von Mosul in der Kgl. Bibliothek zu München." *Münchner Jahrbuch der Bildenden Kunst* 1 (1907): 18–37. (Reprinted in Max van Berchem, *Opera Minora*, 2:1079–98. 2 vols. Geneva: Editions Slatkine, 1978.)

Sadeque, Syedah Fatima. *Baybars I of Egypt*. Dacca: Oxford University Press, 1956. Reprint. New York: AMS Press, 1980.

Al-Ṣafadī. *Al-Wāfī bi'l-wafayāt*. Bibliotheca Islamica, vol. 6 (Die Biographische Lexikon des Ṣalāḥaddīn Ḫalīl Ibn Aibak aṣ-Ṣafadī). 22 vols. to date. Wiesbaden: Franz Steiner Verlag, 1949–.

Ṣā'igh, Sulaymān. *Ta'rīkh al-Mawṣil*. Part I. Cairo: Maṭba'at al-Salafiya, 1342/1923.

Al-Sakkar, Sami. "A Critical Edition of *Tārīkh Irbil* of Ibn al-Mustawfī accompanied by an introduction, evaluation and a biography of the author." Ph.D. diss., University of Cambridge, 1974. (Edition of folios 1–59 only.)

Salām, Muḥammad Zaghlūl. *Ḍiyā' al-Dīn Ibn al-Athīr*. Cairo: Dār al-Ma'ārif, n.d.

Schurmann, H. F. "Mongolian Tributary Practices of the Thirteenth Century." *Harvard Journal of Asiatic Studies* 19 (1956): 304–89.

Sibṭ ibn al-Jawzī. *Mir'āt al-zamān fī ta'rīkh al-a'yān*. Facsimile edition by James Richard Jewett. Chicago: University of Chicago Press, 1907.

Siouffi, N. *Majmū' al-kitābāt al-muḥarrara fī abniyat madīnat al-Mawṣil* (Notes historiques et explicatives sur les inscriptions de la ville de Mossoul). Edited by Sa'īd al-Daywahjī. Baghdad: Maṭba'at Shafīq, 1376/1956. (Based on a nineteenth century manuscript, no. 5142, in the Bibliothèque nationale, Paris.)

Smith, John Masson Jr. "'Ayn Jālūt: Mamlūk Success or Mongol Failure?" *Harvard Journal of Asiatic Studies* 44 (1984): 307–45.

———. "Mongol and Nomadic Taxation." *Harvard Journal of Asiatic Studies* 30 (1970): 46–85.

Spuler, Bertold. *The Mongol Period*. Translated by F. R. C. Bagley. Part 2 of *The Muslim World: A Historical Survey*. Leiden: E. J. Brill, 1969.

Stern, S. M. "A New Volume of the Illustrated Aghānī Manuscript." *Ars Orientalis* 2 (1957): 501–3.

Al-Subkī. *Ṭabaqāt al-shāfi'īya al-kubrā*. Edited by Maḥmūd Muḥammad al-Ṭannāḥī and 'Abd al-Fattāḥ Muḥammad al-Ḥalw. 10 vols. Cairo: 'Īsā al-Bābī al-Ḥalabī, 1964–74.

Al-Suyūṭī. *Ta'rīkh al-khulafā'*. 3rd ed., edited by Muḥammad Muḥyī al-Dīn 'Abd al-Ḥamīd. Cairo: Maṭba'at al-Madanī, 1383/1964.

Thorau, Peter. "The Battle of 'Ayn Jālūt: a Re-examination." In *Crusade and Settlement*, edited by Peter W. Edbury, 236–41. Cardiff: University College Cardiff Press, 1985.

Ṭulaymāt, 'Abd al-Qādir Aḥmad. *Ibn al-Athīr al-Jazarī al-mu'arrikh*. Cairo: Dār al-Kitāb al-Qawmī, 1969.

———. *Muẓaffar al-Dīn Kūkbūrī, Amīr Irbil*. Cairo: Wuzārat al-Thiqāfa wa'l-Irshād al-Qawmī, [1383/1963].

van Berchem, Max. "Monuments et inscriptions de l'atābek Lu'lu' de Mossoul." In *Orientalische Studien Theodor Nöldeke*, edited by Carl Bezold, 1:197–210. Giessen: A. Töpelmann, 1906. (Reprinted in Max van Berchem, *Opera Minora*, 2:659–72. 2 vols. Geneva: Editions Slatkine, 1978.)

Vernadsky, George. *The Mongols and Russia*. Vol. 3 of *A History of Russia*. New Haven: Yale University Press, 1953.

Wickens, G. M. "Nasir ad-Din Tusi on the Fall of Baghdad: A Further Study." *Journal of Semitic Studies* 7 (1962): 23–35.

Al-Yāfi'ī. *Mir'āt al-janān wa-'ibrat al-yaqẓān*. 4 vols. Hyderabad: Dā'ir al-Ma'ārif al-Niẓāmiya, 1337–39/1918–21.

Yāqūt al-Ḥamawī. *The Irshád al-Aríb ilá ma'rifat al-Adíb or Dictionary of Learned Men of Yáqút*. 2nd ed., edited by D. S. Margoliouth. E. J. W. Gibb Memorial Series, vol. 6. 7 vols. London: Luzac and Co., 1923–31.

———. *Kitāb mu'jam al-buldān*. Edited by Ferdinand Wüstenfeld. 6 vols. Leipzig: F. A. Brockhaus, 1866–73. Reprint. Tehran: Maktabat al-Asadī, 1965.

———. *Mu'jām al-udabā'*. Edited by Aḥmad Farīd Rifa'ī. 20 vols. Cairo: Maktabat 'Īsā al-Bābī al-Ḥalabī, 1355/1936.

Al-Yūnīnī. *Dhayl mir'āt al-zamān*. 4 vols. Hyderabad: Osmania Oriental Publications Bureau, 1374–80/1954–61.

Zetterstéen, K. V. "Lu'lu'." *EI*1 3 (1936): 40–41.

Ziada, Mustafa M. "The Mamluk Sultans to 1293." In *The Later Crusades, 1189–1311*, edited by Robert Lee Wolff and Harry W. Hazard, 735–58. Vol. 2 of *A History of the Crusades*. Edited by Kenneth M. Setton. 4 vols. Madison: University of Wisconsin Press, 1969–77.

INDEX

'Abd al-Raḥman, Sultān Shāh 22n, 26n
'Abd al-Razzāq al-Ras'anī, 'Izz al-Dīn b. Rizq Allāh, 68
'Adawiya, 65
Adharbayjān: Hülegü in, 60, 71, 73, 76; Mongol invasion and occupation of, 25n, 26, 32, 52–53
'Adī b. Musāfir, 65
al-'Ādil Abū Bakr, 10–11, 14, 17, 18, 19
al-'Ādil II b. al-Kāmil, 38
al-Afḍal, 8
Aḥmad (Īl-Khānid ruler), 83
'Alā' al-Dīn b. al-Mujāhid Isḥāq, 83
'Alā' al-Mulk b. al-Ṣāliḥ Ismā'īl, 74, 80
Aleppo: 27; contends for control of the Jazira, 39–41, 47; mamluk control of, 75–76; and the Mongols, 56, 71, 73, 75; al-Muẓaffar 'Alī as governor of, 72–73
'Alī b. Abī Ṭālib, 68
'Alī b. Lu'lu', al-Muẓaffar 'Alā' al-Dīn. *See* al-Muẓaffar
'Alids, 50, 68
Amid, 40, 42, 62–63, 71
al-'Amidī, Najīb al-Dīn, 83
Amīn al-Dīn b. Lu'lu', 31, 45, 50
al-Amjad Maḥmūd, 22n
Amṣār, 69
'Āna, 38, 39, 40
Anatolia: Mongols in, 41, 42, 53–54, 60.
Anbār, 77
al-'Aqr, 11, 19, 24, 26
Aqṭāy, Fāris al-Dīn al-Musta'rab, 38n
Aqṭāyā, Fāris al-Dīn, 43
'Arābān, 32, 46n
Arghun, 54, 55n, 56
al-'Arīsh, 85
Armenia, 13, 27, 29, 31, 36
Arslān Shāh, al-'Ādil Nūr al-Dīn b. al-Ṣāliḥ Ismā'īl b. Lu'lu', 71
Arslān Shāh I, Nūr al-Dīn, 8, 9–11, 12–13; 65–67
Arslān Shāh II, Nūr al-Dīn b. Mas'ud, 16, 17, 20, 22
Arslān Shāh III, Nūr al-Dīn b. Zankī, 49–50

ABOUT THE AUTHOR

Douglas Patton received his Ph.D. in Islamic history at New York University. He currently resides in Seattle and is a member of the Middle East Center of the Jackson School of International Studies at the University of Washington.